ON THE
MOVE

ON THE MOVE

A MARINE'S GUIDE TO

ENTREPRENEURIAL SUCCESS

NICK BAUCOM

Published by Advantage, Charleston, South Carolina.
Member of Advantage Media Group.

ADVANTAGE is a registered trademark and the Advantage colophon is a trademark of Advantage Media Group, Inc.

Printed in the United States of America.

ISBN: 978-1-59932-506-4
LCCN: 2014959583

This publication is designed to provide accurate and authoritative information in regard to the subject matter covered. It is sold with the understanding that the publisher is not engaged in rendering legal, accounting, or other professional services. If legal advice or other expert assistance is required, the services of a competent professional person should be sought.

 Advantage Media Group is proud to be a part of the Tree Neutral® program. Tree Neutral offsets the number of trees consumed in the production and printing of this book by taking proactive steps such as planting trees in direct proportion to the number of trees used to print books. To learn more about Tree Neutral, please visit www.treeneutral.com. To learn more about Advantage's commitment to being a responsible steward of the environment, please visit www.advantagefamily.com/green

Advantage Media Group is a publisher of business, self-improvement, and professional development books and online learning. We help entrepreneurs, business leaders, and professionals share their Stories, Passion, and Knowledge to help others Learn & Grow. Do you have a manuscript or book idea that you would like us to consider for publishing? Please visit advantagefamily.com or call 1.866.775.1696.

TABLE OF CONTENTS

ACKNOWLEDGMENTS

This book wouldn't have been possible without my relationships with countless friends, family members, supporters, and organizations. It would take an entire book by itself to list them all, but I just wanted to take a moment to list a few that come to mind.

Dad, thank you for instilling in me the ideals of entrepreneurship by discussing profit margins, brand positioning, and the dynamics of a break-even analysis at an early age as normal dinner conversation.

Mom, thank you for showing me the importance of helping other people and teaching me the difference between right and wrong.

Christy Gutmann, thank you for being a great business partner, friend, and mother to our son. And I would not be where I am without my mentor, Oscar Wiygul, and his guidance and as the "Chairman of our Board."

Andrea Vandersall, a special thanks is due to you for being an inspiring and loyal friend over the years.

I had some crazy times with my three best friends while serving in the Marines in Iraq; thanks for always being there, brothers.

Advantage Media, you've been a great team to work with and helped put all of my thoughts together in a cohesive, well-designed package. Kudos to you.

To my staff of current and former employees…I've got the best job in the world! It's a pleasure to be at the helm of such a group of motivated, dedicated, and committed hard chargers.

To the Marine Corps, I can honestly say that I would not be the man I am today without learning from the wisdom of Marines who came before me and having the opportunity to pass that same wisdom down to younger Marines that are carrying the torch today.

I'd like to dedicate this book to members of our military who gallantly fought for our country and didn't return home. It is up to the rest of us to remember their sacrifice, acknowledge their loss, and live a life of purpose.

INTRODUCTION:

· ·

LEADING
THE PATROL

"All right, Baucom, you're up."

Sgt. Benson's words caught me by surprise. "Yes, sergeant!" I replied, because there was really nothing else to say. "Uh—I'm up for what?" Was it my turn to stand post?

It was June 2003, in the early months of our initial push into Iraq. I was a lance corporal at the time, serving in an infantry unit, and we had occupied a power station.

"You're leading the patrol today," the sergeant said.

My first thought was that others had more experience than I did. I'd never been formally trained to lead a patrol, although I'd participated in plenty of them. But the country, the war, the conditions—it was all new to each one of us. Sure, other guys had put in more time in the service. But we were all facing the same unknowns.

When we would advance to a new location, we'd look for good cover to set up our base of operations. Ideally we would find buildings surrounded by a five- to eight-foot wall. Later in the war, contractors came in and built sprawling bases with air-conditioned mobile homes and airfields. But in 2003, we had none of that. It felt as if we were flying blind, ending up in random locations.

Disorder was the order of the day. The living conditions were dismal. During much of that time, I averaged maybe two hours of sleep a night. We didn't eat well. Our three squads rotated through eight hours when we were up for a patrol, and then eight hours standing post. We had built bunkers of sand bags on all four corners of the power station and hardened the front entrance.

Usually, two of us would stand post for eight hours before rotating to the QRF, or Quick Reaction Force. That meant if the patrol were to take fire, or if our Forward Operating Base got hit, we would be called for immediate backup. That happened a lot. And yet that also was technically our "downtime," when we were on standby. Something was always happening in that downtime, so sleep came seldom.

There are three levels to military missions. The highest is strategic, then operational, then tactical—and that was the level of those who, like me, stood the posts and went on the patrols. Our mission was clear on the tactical level. We knew this was a power station supplying electricity to 150,000 Iraqis. We needed to harden this target.

That much we knew. We didn't concern ourselves with strategic issues, such as how to find those weapons of mass destruction that we thought were real at the time. That was the purview of ranks far higher than mine. For better or worse, the strategic thinkers were the ones who orchestrated the overall picture. At our level, we took care of the tasks at hand.

Sure, I had my own political beliefs. At the time, I supported the US position to go to Iraq. But several years later, when I was called up for a second tour, I told myself I would be going there to fight for my brothers, not for some cause like securing democracy in Iraq. I would be fighting for the man next to me, and he would be fighting for me. It happens in all wars. In the thick of the battle, that's what keeps you going. Patriotism might be why you marched off to war, but you soon see that war isn't glorious.

In Iraq, good training was the difference between life and death—and the Marine training is superb. When I saw those men in action, I knew that without a doubt, the Marine Corps was the finest fighting organization in the world. Those who join are a cut above to begin with, and then they are molded from boot camp onward. They learn infantry and patrol and marksmanship and navigation basics— and they also learn to be leaders. They are taught the principles of good order, honorable conduct, and discipline.

And they learn precision. If you're calling in artillery and mess up the coordinates even slightly, you could drop the artillery on your own unit instead of the enemy. You can't just say, "Sorry, my bad." You have to be on target every single time.

So when Sgt. Benson called me to lead the patrol, I knew that my decisions in the field could determine whether a man would ever return home.

"All right," I told him. "But frankly, I have no idea what I'm doing." I certainly wasn't going to turn down a challenge or an opportunity. And in the Marine Corps, a suggestion is an order. He knew I had as good an idea as anyone could expect.

"I'll walk you through it," the sergeant said. And he did. Step by step, he showed me how to handle the map overlays, the patrol route, the checkpoints, the alternate checkpoints, and the radio frequencies. I learned how to brief the squad and what our immediate action procedures would be if we took contact. I had to make sure everybody had the proper amount of water and ammunition for the patrol.

I'd had briefings about such things, but hearing what to do is one thing and doing it is another. It takes a couple of hours to set up a patrol. You don't just head out with your weapons, walk in a few circles hoping nothing happens, and come back. It takes careful planning. And that's just on the small unit level. Imagine what goes into moving an entire division.

The sergeant was telling me, when he called me up, that it was my time to learn the real deal and to do it now.

PASSING ON THE KNOWLEDGE

We have a duty to pass on and build in others the skills and the abilities and leadership that we have developed, whether in the Marines or in business or in life.

The true measure of your leadership ability is what happens when you're absent—and in Iraq, a leader could be gone in a flash. I like to think that I played a part in making my unit stronger and better, that I developed my Marines. It's not about me or whether I was a great squad leader or platoon sergeant. It's really about that next generation a couple of years behind me. How did they develop as leaders? Did they absorb what they needed to know? Did they, too, pass it on?

In a lot of ways, the corporate world should be envious of the Marine Corps. For more than 200 years, it has built leaders and passed on that *esprit de corps*. A lot of companies fail the test of time. Few are still in business longer than a generation. You seldom hear of a third-generation business. But the Marine Corps has been passing the torch for many generations now.

Sgt. Benson knew what I needed to know, and he was intent on passing it down to me and to all his Marines. He was dedicated to making sure we had the skills and the training and the knowledge to face whatever came our way, and he was showing his trust in me. It was a huge responsibility for anyone, let alone a 19-year-old, and I took it very seriously. I knew there was no room for error.

It can make everything later in life seem like a piece of cake. Anyone running a business has a day now and then when he or she wonders, "Dear God, why am I doing this?" The stresses, one after another, can feel excruciating. And then I think: "Wait a second; I used to sleep on the floor, if I got to sleep at all, for an hour or two at a time. I had no electricity, no plumbing. My family was 6,000 miles away and it was 120 degrees." And suddenly, the stresses of the day fade away.

READY TO TAKE CHARGE

When the job needs to be done, you step up. You don't have a choice. That's the way it is in business, that's the way it is in life—and that certainly was the way it was when I was called to duty in Iraq. I was called up, and I was up to the challenge.

I relished that opportunity to lead the patrol. I didn't want to be a lance corporal forever. When you're called up to the big leagues, so to speak, you just go. "No" isn't an option. You click your heels: "Roger that, Sergeant. Let's do it."

Yes, you can take courses in leadership, but much of it is in the heart and marrow. You must develop proficiency, of course. Authenticity comes from being truly proficient at what you do. You can't fake leadership. People will spot it in a heartbeat if you don't know what you're talking about. So you need to develop abilities beyond those below you—or why would they be following you instead of vice versa?

And yet there is also an aura of leadership that emanates from one's bearing. You have the qualities to be in command of any situation. That's not faking it. I have come to feel I could walk into any room and take charge.

I remember a day near the end of boot camp when the senior drill instructor had a talk with us. We formed a circle around him, and the moment was far more casual than the rigors to which we had become accustomed.

"When you go back home," he said, "and you're back for your 10 days of leave after boot camp, you're going to see all your same friends. They're going to be doing the same things they did when you left. And maybe you'll go to see a movie or something. When you do, you pick the movie, and you pick the time.

"You're a Marine. You're a leader. People are naturally going to follow you, and so you take charge of that situation. You're not going to debate for 30 minutes or an hour on what to do, or let the day slide by and you don't even make it to the movies. You're going to take charge and you're going to make the plan, and you're going to execute it."

That's the spirit that the Marine Corps instills, and it was my operating principle in Iraq on that day when I was called to leadership.

FAST FORWARD

Come with me now to another place and another time, far removed from the Iraqi sands. A decade later finds me growing a booming business in Washington, D.C. called "Two Marines Moving." We help people get on with their lives. We pack up and haul their stuff.

The job on this particular day was challenging, to say the least. The client was a hoarder. The place was piled high with the debris of her life, and she couldn't make up her mind about what she wanted to do—what should stay, and what should go.

The crew had expected to have the truck loaded by 3 o'clock—and the job was still dragging on at 7 o'clock. The crew gave up and came back with the worst attitude, saying they couldn't do this job. They felt demoralized. And so I went upstairs and I put on our company uniform and boots and I came down and I gave them a proper ass-chewing.

"You know what, there's nothing here I wouldn't do myself, even as the owner of this company," I told the crew. "I will not ask you to do anything that I haven't done myself. I've been out on late jobs lots of times. It was snowing and 20 degrees on the first move I ever did with this company. Anything I ask you to do, I've done myself."

They told me they saw my point and offered to go back out, but I told them to go home. This was serious. I got one of my office personnel to assist, and we went out to finish the move. I was at the client's house until 10 o'clock and got the job done. I wanted to drive home the lesson.

The crew knew that I meant what I said. It wasn't some BS speech, the kind some bosses give, that "we're all in this together." I had my boots on. I kept a promise. The crew saw that. The job needed to be done, without excuses, and the crew needed to see what leadership was all about.

Today, the chief of that crew is my training chief, responsible for showing all the employees what is expected of them. I guarantee you he remembers that leadership lesson. Daniel Correa was a noncommissioned officer in the Marine Corps, and he proved his potential. He is a leader, and people follow him. He and the crew had a bad day with that particular client, but I held him to a higher level than the others. The troops will follow the leader's example, and those who follow you will rise to your level of expectation.

Each of us must be held accountable. I hold others accountable, and others hold me accountable—and that's a principle in both the Marine Corps and in business. As a leader in the Corps, you have two primary responsibilities: (1) complete the mission; and (2) take care of your troops. And holding them accountable is part of taking care of them.

STANDING TALL

Ask any Marine if he's ever gone on a 20-mile "hump," and you'll hear a story right away. Civilians would call them hikes—and they are agonizing. I've done dozens of them. You carry over 100 pounds of gear at a brisk pace. You get only two or three breaks. You have to be in peak condition.

Sometimes, in the middle of it, you're wondering, "Why did I do this to myself? Why did I join the infantry? I could be in an office having an easy day. I wouldn't be slogging up and down hills. I wouldn't be sleeping under the stars on a 10-degree night."

But then you march back on base, and you're going past the PX, and you see the visiting parents and kids. You're in full gear, with weapons, and they are looking in awe at this infantry battalion passing by. On that last mile, you stand tall, and you push out your chest. This is what people make movies about, and you're doing it in real life. You made it through. It's like finishing a marathon.

It felt more as if I were starting a marathon on that day in Iraq when I was ordered to lead the patrol. I laid out the mission and the destinations. I wrote down the checkpoints. I learned the proper procedures if I were to perceive any threats. I mapped out alternatives.

I made sure that all my Marines had the necessary gear and water and ammunition and that their weapons were clean and ready. We practiced hand and arm signals. I drilled my Marines on proper spacing and alignment to limit how many could be hit by one grenade. I reviewed how to call in a casualty report.

I also had an assistant patrol leader, who had to know these things as well, and everybody on the team had to be thoroughly briefed and take notes. What would happen, say, if Brown were hit and couldn't operate the radio? What if we needed to call for an air strike—who would handle communications?

Everybody on the team had to understand the mission. We went over it twice. We identified it precisely—and also made sure to explain the "why"—we were doing it "in order to" accomplish what. For example: "Our mission is to take this bridge. This is a strategic gateway into the city. We will take this position and defend it in order to allow a third platoon to bypass this route and go to the municipal building, the mayor's headquarters."

Let's say Smith thinks his job is to hold his gun and look out for the bad guys, but then he sees an enemy force moving toward the mayor's house. He knows that, in the overall picture, the third platoon is heading to that position. He needs to let me, as the squad leader, know what he has observed so that I can apprise the commanding officer and we can adapt, improvise, and overcome.

Smith's input could change the entire scheme of maneuver, so we have to be able to pivot quickly to accomplish our goals. There are many trees in the forest. Smith knows his part of the mission—his particular tree—but he also knows it's part of the forest. The Marine Corps is saying, "Every single person involved in this mission is important and has a direct contribution to the final outcome. It is important that everyone knows the mission."

I use that principle today in my business. I can't always tell people the reason we do everything, but I always try to give them the why. What's the bigger picture behind this? That way they can think for themselves as opposed to just waiting for my orders.

The men were waiting for my orders that day in Iraq. This was my call to leadership. This was my moment to stand tall.

THE BIRTH OF A BUSINESS

After I left the service and was ready to launch my civilian life, it was time for me to lead another kind of patrol. Once again, I was up for the challenge—and once again, I didn't know at first just how I was going to do it. I just knew that I could.

As I assessed my life and career plans, I found myself getting a lot of calls and texts from friends and family: "Hey, Nick, could you come over to help me move?" Later, I'd invariably hear a comment like this: "Sure glad we've got a strong Marine here to help us out."

I thought, "All right, there's something to this. I'm not going to do this for beer and pizza anymore." I had recently moved to Washington, D.C., and had wanted to start some sort of business there. It occurred to me that I could start a profitable moving company.

That's how Two Marines Moving was born. I started the business on the birthday of the Marine Corps, which was established in 1775. I registered the website the evening of November 10, 2008, and built it in the next three or four days. I had my first job and first employee the next week. Today, we operate in a 60-mile radius of Washington, D.C. We do long-distance moves as well, but they have to originate in the D.C. area. We've moved people as far as Florida and California and Canada.

"I'm going to have $10,000 in the bank in four months," I told Christy, my wife at the time and still my business partner, when I launched the business.

"No way," she said. "This is risky. You're starting a business. Nobody has a profitable business the first year. Give it time. It'll come."

"That might be what people think," I said, "but that's not what's going to happen."

It was only a couple months later that I had $10,000 extra in the bank to buy a truck, do marketing, and get office space. The first year in business we did more than $600,000 in revenue. The next year we doubled that, to $1.2 million. The year after that, we did

$2.4 million. In 2013, we did $3.4 million. As I write this, we are projecting more than $4 million for 2014.

I launched Two Marines Moving when I was 24, and within a few years we were on *Inc.* magazine's list of fastest growing companies—and a lot of those were technology companies. It's spectacular for a local moving company to have that kind of growth rate and to be among that elite.

I had been reading *Inc.* since I was a teenager. "One day," I had told myself, "I will be featured in this magazine. I will be on that list." It had been a dream. The magazine held a gala for us, and when I met the others in that peer group, it was immensely gratifying. I had the same feeling of pride and accomplishment as when I'd been pinned with the Eagle, Globe, and Anchor by earning the title Marine upon the completion of boot camp.

I was 25 the year that we hit $1.2 million dollars in revenue. A lot of companies are bought out for one-time their revenue, and so technically I could have been considered a millionaire at that age, in terms of net worth. I chose not to sell my company because one day I'll make that much in profit.

Why did I name my company Two Marines Moving? The word "moving" clearly needed to be part of the name, to identify what we did—always a good idea, but particularly critical for search engine optimization.

And why "two?" Certainly, when I named the company, I knew that I would have far more than two employees. A fellow student at the University of Memphis once told me that no matter what I did in life, I was an "empire builder," and I liked the sound of that. And yet I always will want the small-business touch and feel. I wanted to use the number two to communicate that this wasn't some faceless organization, whether we were 10 employees or 100 or 1,000.

Today, you're still going to get two Marines showing up to your door, even if you'll eventually need an entire platoon to move your home or office. Our logo—two Marines at attention, flanking a truck—communicates the honor and dependability of the Corps. I also wanted to show that this is always going to be a personable operation. It's about relationships and referrals and repeat business. We will not become a big company just for the sake of being a big company.

LESSONS TO SHARE

I turned 30 as I wrote this book. Not that long ago, I was a 19-year-old leading that patrol in Iraq. Today's mission, though quite different, is an important one nonetheless. I am in the business of helping people and serving them, and that is a fulfilling and satisfying endeavor.

In my transition from military to civilian life, I have learned so much—and I have found meaningful and productive ways to apply the Marine Corps traits and principles that have become part of the definition of Nick Baucom. My goal is to show others how to take their base talents and abilities and interests and apply them to entrepreneurial pursuits that will be perfect for them.

Military experience is a good preparation not only for business leadership but also for life itself, and for parenthood. It seems many parents don't pay much attention to their children's choice of friends. Christy and I have a 5-year-old son, Isaac. He's a joy, and he respects me and he respects his mom. We're his life now. But as he gets older, he'll be spending more time with his peers than he will with us. So you'd better believe I'll be keeping a close watch on who is influencing him.

He will need to understand the consequences of the things that he and his friends do, for better or worse. I love him deeply, but I'm not there to be his best friend. I'm there to be his dad, a strong father figure. My job is to hold him accountable. That's the nature of leadership.

In this book, I will be telling you my story, and in so doing you will see how my military experience has contributed greatly to my entrepreneurial success. I know that many of you who are reading these words are military personnel or veterans who are wondering, "What's next?" I hope to show you a world of possibilities. I hope to help launch you into the full potential of your leadership.

Perhaps you are dreaming of starting a business, or you are getting one under way and are looking for guidance. Maybe you find yourself working two jobs to stay above water, or you have found your business pursuits to be unbearably frustrating.

I see a lot of business owners who, in effect, have bought themselves a job. They're doing $3 million a year in revenue, but they're killing themselves to get that. They're making $60,000 a year in profit, but they're working 70-hour weeks and feel as if they're about to have a coronary.

How, then, do they move to the next level? How do they double their profit to $120,000 and beyond and get to the point where they can take vacations whenever they want, plan for the future, and not feel oppressed by the many struggles and stresses of owning and running the business?

You're dreaming of freedom and autonomy. You want to be your own man, or your own woman—and those rewards should come naturally for an entrepreneur. Let me show you how I made that leap. My hope is that it will encourage you and empower you to make such a leap yourself.

FOLLOWING A GOOD EXAMPLE

This is not a book full of business operations and procedures. Those are important, and I've learned them along the way, mostly through my own reading and my experiences in the Marines.

Rather, this is a book of fundamental principles and required rules for success. This is a book of inspiration and encouragement. I know how frustration feels. I know the pain of failure. Let me tell you up front: I have fallen on my face. I lost a business once, and I will be telling you about that in the pages ahead. I don't want to repeat that experience.

I have learned that what's most important in running a business is to know yourself—who you are, what motivates you, what drives you to success—and to develop your leadership abilities. And that doesn't come from a business degree.

In no way am I putting down those who have invested in an MBA. Certainly, much can be learned in classrooms. But so much of success comes from trial and error. It's about making mistakes and then correcting yourself so you don't make them again. It's about learning from others.

In business, as in so much else in life, it's about observing your peers and following the good examples and staying the hell away from the bad ones. The Marine Corps drilled that into me. We were warned to stay away from the losers on the street corners back home. "They're not going anywhere in life," our mentors said, "so be careful who you hang around with. You don't even want to be around that set. You're different now. You're a Marine."

It doesn't make you perfect. Getting that Eagle, Globe and Anchor itself doesn't transform you, but the culture instills the desire to excel for those who take it seriously. Some don't make it. But many enlistees become highly competitive and driven to succeed.

Yes, an MBA is extremely valuable, but life is bigger than that. If you were to interview the top leaders in any industry, do you think they would say, "This is what made me so successful—it's because I can analyze this cash flow statement in 30 seconds."

I suspect that, instead, they would talk about leadership, and the ability to improvise, adapt, and overcome. You would hear about how they look out for the troops. Sure, leaders need to know their stuff. But success is more about being made of the right stuff.

THE TACTICAL AND THE STRATEGIC

What I offer you here is a foundation—one that must be in place before you can build on it all those technical details. I think back to my Marine training: Yes, I know the tactical side. I know what my employees need to know, and I pass it on to them. But it's the strategic side upon which I am building a business and a future.

They go hand-in-hand. The big picture governs the details, certainly—but it's also true that in the details, you see a reflection of the big picture.

When I arrive at my office each day, I glance at the vending machine, and not because I've skipped breakfast. Among the duties that I have given to my dispatchers—it's on their weekly checklist— is to make sure that vending machine is stocked.

Things can get very busy at the office, with a lot of people coming and going. A glance at that vending machine tells me a lot about the big picture. If the vending machine isn't stocked, something's wrong at my company. It's a small detail, but it could mean that we don't have enough office staff—our troop-to-task ratio is off. If one detail goes unattended, then I know other details are being overlooked.

Yes, it's just a vending machine. But it's also symptomatic of the overall health of my company at that moment. This is both a tactical and strategic matter.

Long ago, miners would keep a canary in the coalmine as a test for deadly gases. Canaries are very sensitive to oxygen levels, much more so than are humans. If the canary went belly up, they knew something was very wrong up ahead. In our businesses, in our families, in our lives, each of us must have a canary. It's a little thing, but it chirps loudly. It speaks volumes about what leaders need to know.

My vending machine, likewise, serves that purpose. Paying close attention to it is not the whim of a petty boss. It's a way of protecting the troops—and the business that sustains them.

MARINE PRINCIPLES AND TRAITS

Throughout this book, in every chapter, you will be learning about the Marine Corps principles and traits of leadership. You will see many of them in action as you read these pages.

Those are the guidelines for becoming a good Marine. They were drilled into us. Some things I heard endlessly during my six years of service. Even a slight slip was called to our attention: "Baucom! Straighten that belt! Adjust that ribbon!" Most people don't notice such things. Marines do. We are tuned to detail.

In squad leader school, a big sign hung at the front of the classroom: "Follow me." That's the school's slogan. What it communicates is that a leader does not just stand in the background barking,

"Do this, do that!" Not at all. If a building is full of insurgents, guess who will be first to step toward it? The squad leader. I was in that role. "Follow me," I said, and my Marines did just that.

Adapt, improvise, overcome! I heard it hundreds of times. We didn't just endure what some might see as nitpicking over a uniform violation. A good Marine can tell you about lessons learned from the Corps's official list of traits and principles—and about many others learned along the way.

In short, Marines learn how not to fail in the field. And, in short, that's what I want to share with you, whether or not you have spent time in the service. These are rules for everyone, and they are good for the long haul.

CHAPTER 1:

· ·

SUMMER BREAK
IN BAGHDAD

The room clearly had been used as a torture cell. I felt as if I were witness to the aftermath of some unspeakable atrocity, such as the liberating troops saw in Berlin or Auschwitz. This was the work of Saddam's secret police.

We were at the Republican Guard barracks in Al-Kut, Iraq, about 60 miles south of Baghdad. Our battalion cleared out the entire facility and then took it over as our own. We set up shop there, so to speak.

First, we went through each and every building looking for important paperwork, all the while keeping our eyes open for any bad guys in green uniforms—and, of course, those WMDs, weapons of mass destruction. The proper method for clearing a room is called doing a button hook and a cross, either a squad-size element in the building or a platoon-size element.

In one of the rooms, we saw the telltale tools of the torture trade—knives of various creative styles, and all manner of blunt instruments of pain.

We saw the cylinders that the tormentors would insert under toenails and fingernails to pop them off. We saw broomsticks used to pummel the bottoms of people's feet. The objective wasn't death. The objective was blinding pain. Saddam's henchmen were known to push people off four-story roofs, not high enough to kill them, but certainly high enough to shatter femurs and shins. The victims would live to warn others. Here, in this special room, chairs had been set up for those selected for these treatments, and, as we immediately observed, there had been blood.

In one of the rooms, we saw the telltale tools of the torture trade—knives of various creative styles, and all manner of blunt instruments of pain.

Out in the city center, where we were sent out on patrol, we later saw videos for sale in the market. The Iraqi kids would sell them for a dollar, promising hours and hours of torture sessions. We saw sights in the city that will linger a lifetime. I met one Iraqi when I was on a post in Al-Kut who was trying to communicate to me with his hands. He had no tongue. He obviously had offended someone in power.

The danger doesn't always come from the enemy, or from enemy fire. Serving in the military involves the inherent risk that arises when a lot of people are around a lot of weaponry and heavy equipment. On my fourth day in Iraq, I was walking past the command headquarters. Suddenly, only 50 or 60 feet from me, something exploded. This was in relatively a safe location. It turned out that a Navy Seabee had picked up on old Iraqi mortar shell—he should never have done that—and was getting ready to show his peers how it worked, how to take it apart. He was disassembling it with his Gerber tool when the explosion disassembled him.

I was among those tasked with getting his body parts together so that his remains could be sent home for the funeral. A few of his fingers had blown right past my face. It was a lesson that I never wanted to forget—even if I could.

THE HORROR, THE BOREDOM

One morning as I was standing post in al-Hayy, letting our vehicles in and out, I met a little girl named Ellah. It was about 11 a.m. and already 110 degrees. We'd had our daily briefing, and we were alerted to watch out for an orange-and-white stolen vehicle that was to be used as a car bomb. (Many vehicles in the city were orange and white, designating a car for hire. They're as ubiquitous as yellow cabs in New York.)

This little girl came over with a friend, pointing at her bandaged arm. I could understand that her name was Ellah, and that she wanted help, but not much else—except that the expression of pain on a human face is universal. I knew this child was no threat.

"Let me take a look at it," I said. I gently unwrapped the bandage, expecting to see the red and brown of bloodstains. The wound was green. She had been injured for many days. I called for a medic, and as he cleaned the infection, Ellah told us—with the help of her friend, who knew a few words of English—that she had been hit by a mortar blast.

Ellah was perhaps 8 years old, a child caught up in war and politics who understood none of it—nothing of al-Qaeda or Saddam or the elusive WMDs. She was a little girl, with a bandaged arm. A decade later, I have a little boy now. His name is Isaac, and he's 5 years old. I want for him a better world.

We all witnessed such horrors, and endured days of little sleep and awful food—and mind-numbing boredom. We would get up at 1 a.m. to stand an eight-hour post until 9 a.m. Once we were relieved it would be back to our racks, just to get up again for QRF. War is 99 percent boredom and 1 percent action. People think of the choppers and the bombings and the attacks. Such is war, of course, but much of the time it seems like a relentless nothingness.

Most every Marine wants to see action. As a whole, they crave it. They've trained for years to go to war—and if they don't get to fight, it can feel like being on a football team that lets you practice but keeps you benched, never lets you in the game.

They often end up feeling that they didn't do enough. You hear stories of Marines who jumped on a grenade or who were in the Battle of Fallujah. I personally don't feel like I did enough. But even those Marines who were in Fallujah would say pretty much the same thing. We have a lot of reverence for our fallen brothers. They truly gave everything, and somehow anything less feels like falling short.

Marines are trained to kill, but that doesn't make them killing machines. Many of these men and women have children at home. They are compassionate souls. When they fight, it's out of duty. They do what they must. Once, when I was at the scene of a potential riot, a huge Iraqi—probably 6 foot 5 and 250 pounds of solid muscle—

grabbed my weapon as we were pushing people back. I did a quick defensive maneuver with my weapon, as we were taught to do in such cases. With my rifle in his face, I shouted at him in Arabic to step back or die. He listened.

That was a case where his life was literally in my hands. You don't grab a Marine's weapon with impunity. It's no time for negotiations. Under our guidelines and rules of engagement, I had every right to shoot him. But I didn't. Unless you're a sociopath, you don't jump at a chance to take someone's life. It's necessary at times, certainly, but not natural.

FACING THE FEAR

Bravery abounds, but it doesn't mean you are immune to fear. Some of those kids were truly frightened. I remember one who was under my command when I was slated to go back to Iraq for a second tour, several years later. "Sgt. Baucom," he asked me, "do you think I'm going to die?"

"Well," I said, pulling him aside, "you might die. You might not." What else can a man say? War is random. I couldn't say, "There, there, fear not: I'll bring you home safe and sound, no matter what."

No matter how well trained you are, no matter how good you are, you might be the one who steps on the wrong square foot of soil—one that has an IED underneath it. Your foot hits the trip plate, and you're gone. It might have no bearing on how alert you were. Life and death can be that arbitrary.

"I can only tell you that you're a well-trained Marine," I told that young man. If I had said, "No, you're not going to die," what kind of respect would I have instilled in him? He knew he could die. I told him how it was. His exceptional training raised his odds of living dramatically. It's horrible that we lost nearly 4,500 troops in Iraq, but the United States deployed 2.5 million troops to the region since going to war with Afghanistan in 2001. Statistically, he would survive his tour.

"We're here for one another," I told him. "You're prepared, you know how to deal with situations, how to keep your eyes open. You're with the band of your brothers. But listen: You joined the infantry. You're the tip of the spear. We're on the frontlines for a reason. Hell, we're what it's all about—everybody else moves in support of us. At the end of the day, you will be able to say, 'I did something incredible. I took part in something that changed politics and changed this country, changed our country.'"

Whether in war or in business, leadership cannot entail false optimism. The leader's job is to encourage, certainly, but if you're bright-eyed about situations that clearly are troubling, you will lose respect. When my junior Marines complained about the humps, I'd tell them: "All right. It's going to suck. We know it. Let's do it, to the best of our abilities, and get it done. In four hours, it's going to be over."

You can't bullshit someone and say, "This is going to be so much fun. I'm going to enjoy trekking around for eight hours with all that gear on." People can see right through you. Nobody wants to be manipulated. I'm a big believer in just saying how it is, and that's how the cards are, and that's what we'll work with. That promotes clarity. That's how you build respect and get the job done.

I enrolled at the University of Memphis right after finishing my training at the School of Infantry. I had joined the Reserves so that I could serve my country while also pursuing personal endeavors, such as going to college. The Reserves, I'd been told, would require only one weekend a month and two weeks a year of my time. I checked into my unit, and I'd gone through one drill.

Then came the call from my platoon sergeant: "Is this PFC Baucom? This is Sgt. Tinsley. Our unit is going to Iraq." It was March 2003, and the United States was leading the invasion. I had five days to drop everything in civilian life and report for duty. College would have to wait. I wouldn't be back in the States until August—just in time to resume classes for the fall semester.

I remember sitting in an English class on the first day as the students were introducing themselves. Since it was the fall semester, they mostly talked about their summer doings. They reported on how much they had learned in their internships, or they glowed about family cruises and great parties. Some related the rigors of pledging to a fraternity or sorority.

I felt a weak smile coming to my face as I thought about my own recent past. How would I ever find the words to describe my summer? Would I tell them that I had bagged a man's fingers and toes? Would I describe how I crawled into a torture chamber? Would I tell them about a little girl named Ellah with a green, infected arm?

These were my peers, but I felt so little in common with them anymore. Still, I was happy for my classmates. They were home living their regular lives—and that's what it's all about. Throughout history, that's why people have gone off to fight in wars, so that those back home can lead normal lives. They can go to their classes, and to their jobs; they can fall in love and raise families; they can start businesses and plan for their future.

I had seen some of mankind's worst in Iraq, but I also had seen the best. It was my privilege to serve with my brothers there. I've remained particularly close with four of my fellow Marines, and I know they'd take a bullet for me to this day, as I would for them.

You form bonds that can be stronger than blood. Our very lives depended on our being there for one another, and when things got tough, it was for one another we fought. We weren't thinking about America and apple pie. "Greater love has no one than this: to lay down one's life for one's friends"—I heard those words in church, and I know now in my heart that they are true.

When I joined the Marines, I knew I was doing so during a time of war. But at that point, the Reserves hadn't been called up since the Persian Gulf War of 1990–91. I knew it could happen, but I didn't think it would be so soon. After boot camp and infantry school, I had been home only a month or so when we got the call to mobilize.

"Greater love has no one than this: to lay down one's life for one's friends"—I heard those words in church, and I know now in my heart that they are true.

During my six years in the Reserves, I ended up doing three years of active duty. I was a lance corporal when I was in Iraq and later a sergeant. Only about half of Marines make corporal, and of those, only half make sergeant—so I felt that I was among the top tier. It turned out to be a commitment far deeper and longer than one weekend a month and a few weeks each year.

Four years after that scorching summer of '03, I was struggling on a number of fronts in my civilian life as I tried to launch into the world of the entrepreneur. I was beginning to learn how those

Marine Corps principles were a great guide for civilian life, as well—and should be a model for business leadership. One day, my phone rang, and these were the words I heard: "We're going back to Iraq."

CHAPTER 2:

· ·

DEALING AND WHEELING

The teacher was scowling. "Nick, open your desk. What do you have in there?" I slowly lifted the desktop to reveal the goods that I had been dealing to my classmates.

There, arranged for sale, were several hundred sports cards—baseball, basketball, football—and X-men cards, too. This was suburban Memphis, 1994. I was 9 years old and in the fifth grade.

I knew my market and the top commodities of the day. The Chicago Bulls were huge. Memphis is a basketball town, so Michael Jordan was hot, and Scottie Pippen, Steve Kerr, Dennis Rodman. In football, Emmitt Smith. In baseball, Darryl Strawberry.

I had separated the best cards for individual sale. That's where the profit was. It wasn't in buying a pack for $2 and reselling it for maybe a slight markup. No, I'd take them apart to find the stars. I probably had a profit margin of 100 or 200 percent. I was making $50 or $60 a day selling cards.

LEARNING FROM A VET

It was my grandfather who had led me to this. Edmond Otto Baucom was an Army veteran who had been at Pearl Harbor when it was attacked. I know that experience had contributed to shaping my Pappaw into the man he was.

I got out of school every December 7 to go with him to a Pearl Harbor survivors gathering. When I was 5 or 6 years old, those meetings filled a huge banquet hall. Several hundred attended. When I was 20 and fresh back from Iraq, I was keynote speaker—and only about 70 people were there. I told them how much the sacrifice of my grandfather and his generation meant to those of us carrying that torch today.

I remember Pappaw's stories of that day in Honolulu when the Japanese planes began strafing and bombing. The ammunition had been locked up, so he ended up being given a .45-caliber pistol at the armory with eleven rounds—and that was his defense against the four-hour attack that morning. He didn't talk about it much, but I recall him describing how a Zero plane had strafed him, riddling the ground around him, as the harbor erupted in explosions. Had just one bullet succeeded, I wouldn't be writing this today.

My grandfather was an Iowa farm boy who had volunteered to serve. As the USS Arizona burned in the harbor, his family was back home, tending to the cows. He had joined the service in '39—when he was 18, the age at which I would join more than six decades later. Both of us joined during peacetime but soon found ourselves ushered into war. He knew what I would come to know.

And he also knew the value within a pack of sports cards.

My grandfather didn't talk about it much, but I recall him describing how a Zero plane had strafed him, riddling the ground around him, as the harbor erupted in explosions. Had just one bullet succeeded, I wouldn't be writing this today.

Pappaw would pick me up at school every day, and he and Gram would watch out for me at their house. On the way home, we would pass the Tennessee Card Company. We stopped one day, and I bought some packs of cards. I took them to school the next day to show them off.

"Hey, I'll buy that card from you for a dollar," one kid offered. I had paid $1.10 for the entire pack, and he was paying me a dollar for just one card? "Well, this is obvious," I thought.

My grandfather, impressed, took me back the next day to reinvest my profits. I had $6 in my pocket from the previous day, so I bought five packs, took them apart and found the good ones—and the next day I made $3 or $4 for each pack. It was like a daily double, and the card company became a routine stop.

SEIZING THE OPPORTUNITY

I ended up dedicating my desk to my business, rather than to my studies. When the teacher noticed that I was a hub of commerce of some sort, and made me show her what lay within, she didn't see any homework or books or rulers. She saw my inventory.

But she wasn't seeing the half of it. Back at my house, I had expanded the business. It was my second location. The kids I played with in my neighborhood were also good prospects for sales, and so I set up shop in our backyard shed. I set up a display case. The kids would come in, look over the cards, and go home and ask their parents for a dollar or five dollars, which would end up in my pocket.

I even hired a security guard. That's what stores at the mall did, and that's how it was on TV, so I figured I'd better get professional here, too. In return for some choice picks of my inventory, my friend Joseph agreed to stand guard at the shop and only let people in two at a time. I set up my Battleship game and put in a pin every time I had a sale. It was the next best thing to a laptop. I figured every businessman should have a laptop, but in 1994 those things cost $5,000.

I have come to believe that we learn and grow from the failures we experience. It's true in life, and it's true in business, and my grade-school entrepreneurial enterprise was in jeopardy. I was suspended from school for disrupting class. I certainly wasn't focusing on my studies, and neither were the other kids—they were busy showing off the cards they had just bought from me.

"Why would you do such a thing?" the teacher asked. And I thought, "Well, why wouldn't I?" I was 9 years old and making more in a day than kids a decade older made in a minimum wage job. This was some real money. And my grades weren't all that bad. I was getting Bs. I wasn't ever a straight-A student. I was getting all my work done.

Even at that age, I was incredibly bored by academics and fascinated by entrepreneurship. The cash register was ringing in my head: "Hmm, $50 a day, times a 180-day school year—I can get rich!" I may not have been the best of students, but I was curious and ambitious. Something inside me wanted to run a business. I seized the opportunity. And that drive is with me today.

"Why would you do such a thing?" the teacher asked. And I thought,
"Well, why wouldn't I?" I was 9 years old and making more in a day
than kids a decade older made in a minimum wage job.

Entrepreneurs think differently. I know I did. I struggled in
Spanish. "You want to be an entrepreneur?" the teacher told me.
"Well, you need to know Spanish. It's the future. This country, as it
diversifies, it's a potentially huge market." And she was right. But at
16, my unspoken thought was this: "Frankly, I'll hire someone as a
translator if I need one. What might that cost, $20 an hour? If I'm in
a situation where I'll be brokering a deal in Latin America, my time
will be worth a lot more than that." Yes, to speak a foreign language
is a valuable asset. But entrepreneurs think naturally in terms of delegating tasks and the value of their time. It's not condescension. It's
business.

LOVING SUPPORT

I had what you might call a vanilla childhood, for which I am
grateful. My parents—Phil and Charlotte Baucom—were supportive
and loved me, and I always knew that. But life almost seems prede-
termined in Memphis. Students were led to believe that it was like
the pinnacle of success if you got your degree at the University of
Memphis and went to work for FedEx. That just sounded humdrum
and boring to me, although I respect my father's 20 years at FedEx.
He was a driver and dispatcher and became the company's safety
instructor.

He's a smart guy, and he tried his hand at his own business when I was a little kid, 5 or 6 years old. His business acumen is good but it didn't work out for him—and I certainly know how that feels, as I later would find out first hand. But he had been willing to take a risk, and he instilled that in me.

"Charlotte, let it go," he told my mother when I was suspended from school. "No big deal. Nick got suspended for being an entrepreneur. This isn't like he was dealing drugs at school. It was baseball cards." My mother felt I should get a good talking to. My father was more inclined to talk to me about my good profit margin.

> My mother felt I should get a good talking to. My father was more inclined to talk to me about my good profit margin.

My mother was a guidance counselor and a violence prevention and drug counselor for the Memphis School District. She always worked with at-risk kids, whether 5-year-olds or 18-year-olds. She had seen many children who had been sidelined in life, or who were heading the wrong way. She certainly wanted her son to be successful. She wanted to see me in college. But she didn't want me to be at risk as an entrepreneur.

"Why don't you just get a job?" I remember her saying at one point. "You could get a position at FedEx." My mother's advice, I know, came from love and concern. But a job at FedEx just wasn't for me. I didn't want to be an employee at FedEx. I wanted to be like Fred Smith, the company's CEO, who founded FedEx at age 27 after two tours as a Marine in Vietnam. He raised $91 million ($525 million in today's dollars), a record at that time.

As a young entrepreneur myself, I can relate to what he must have gone through. I've been told more than once that I'm "too big for my britches." I'm proud of my multimillion-dollar success with Two Marines Moving. How did I do it? For one thing, you can't listen to the naysayers.

My dad instilled in me a passion for entrepreneurship and a respect for business leaders who create jobs, and I'll forever be grateful. Together, my parents shaped me into a man who will take risks but who balances them with a dose of reality. Entrepreneurs must take calculated risks—or how will they ever accomplish anything?

I never met Fred Smith, but unbeknown to him, he had an impact on my life.

A BUDDING BUSINESSMAN

Certainly, my parents had seen my own success as a young businessman. I had mowed yards from age 13 until I graduated from high school. At 16, I was expected to buy my own car if I wanted one. I'm still not sure whether my parents couldn't or wouldn't. They were proud when I was able to do so on my own—although my mother wasn't happy that it was a Camaro Z28 with 300-something horsepower. But it was my money. It was $12,000 that I had saved from mowing yards.

Together, my parents shaped me into a man who will take risks but who balances them with a dose of reality. Entrepreneurs must take calculated risks—or how will they ever accomplish anything?

I'd launched that business three years earlier. My family had been paying a guy named Brooks $35 or $40 to mow our yard. He came with a team of three people and they'd be done in 15 minutes. I said to myself, "Wow! $35 in fifteen minutes?" Brooks invited his neighborhood clients to a party at his place in the neighboring county—and he owned a mansion complete with a pond and pool. "I can do what he does," I told myself. "If he can live like this just by mowing yards, I want a piece of that action."

I got a loan from my grandfather to buy a mower and pitched my argument to my parents: "Let's keep the money in the family, what do you say?" And then I went door-to-door, building the business. I ended up with about 30 clients, and every spring I'd get more. I paid a few of my friends $10 an hour to mow. I got the contracts and did the spin trimming, making the edges right. They did the mowing.

I even had to deal with labor-relations issues. One mom was upset that I was keeping more money for myself than I was paying her son. I told her that nothing was stopping him from drumming up his own clients if he wanted to start a business, but if he worked for me and used my equipment, he would earn the going rate.

The winnings go to the bold and to those willing to take risks. I saw the possibilities and took action. I sold those cards. I mowed those yards and built that business. I didn't just think about what might be and say "maybe later." I got off my ass and actually did it. And that's how I came to be driving my Camaro to school as I waved to my friends on the yellow bus.

Today, I'm sure people sometimes look at me and figure I can't be making much as a mover guy. The moving business isn't glamorous. But I live in a penthouse. Making money is not about the line of work. It's almost better if you are involved in an unattractive line of work that people don't want to do. You have less competition. There are millions of opportunities out there, and you don't have to develop an app to build your dream. After all, bringing a high level of integrity and customer to an industry sorely lacking it is pretty low hanging fruit.

I saw the possibilities and took action. I sold those cards. I mowed those yards and built that business. I didn't just think about what might be and say "maybe later." I got off my ass and actually did it.

What drives me—what has always driven me—is the spirit of entrepreneurship itself. That can be expressed in many pursuits, and I've tried my hand at quite a few. I have learned lessons from life and from military service that can help to deliver success. Those who become entrepreneurs and who become Marines share a personality trait: They tend to be restless, with high energy. Let's focus that power.

So much of success is about getting up and doing the work. You need results, and that comes from taking action. What matters to a business owner is the sale. I see a lot of business owners and wannabe business owners who focus on everything but getting the sale. They'll ask me for advice about what logo looks best, or whether they should get a nice truck, or how they should classify the staff. Sure, those are important questions, but what they need to be thinking about mostly is putting money in the bank. Those details do matter, but they can't stop you from moving forward. It can be scary to start a business. I get it. But you can't bury yourself in the details to avoid the tough work of putting yourself out there, asking for business, and not stopping until you get it. So go door to door and keep at it until you've signed up ten clients, and then impress the hell out of them.

What matters to the business owner is the sale. You can't bury your-self in the details to avoid the tough work of putting yourself out there, asking for business, and not stopping until you get it.

THE BOOKS FROM THE GARAGE

Recently, while my parents were cleaning out the garage, they found my books, 20 boxes of them, and they knew better than to put them out with the trash. These were the books I read as a teenager before heading off to boot camp, and the titles reflect my interests from about age 13 on up.

Every good book is worth reading again—the lessons inside them are just as valuable today as they were then—and so my parents packed them all up and shipped them to me in Washington, D.C. I haven't lost the reading habit. In fact, one reason I chose my home was that it was next door to a Barnes & Noble bookstore.

The books that they sent to me included, to name a few: *The Ernst & Young Guide to Taking Your Company Public*; *Beyond Entrepreneurship*; *Lessons from the eFront*; *Inside Yahoo!*; *The Wal-Mart Decade*; and profiles on Michael Dell of Dell Inc., Jeff Bezos of Amazon, Fred Smith of FedEx, and Dave Thomas of Wendy's. I was reading quite a few books on war and military history, as well, such as *Campaign at Guadalcanal*, in which my grandfather took part. Other titles: *Accept No Mediocre Life*, *Becoming Better Leaders*, and *Brand Simple*.

Looking over those titles today, I'm reminded of how hungry I was to make something of myself. Many of those books are about people who built empires, who have national and international footprints. I was drawn to that. I read voraciously—*The Washington Post, INC Magazine, Wall Street Journal, Fast Company.* I was on a quest for knowledge.

AN ITCH TO ENLIST

I was also on a quest for experience. Joining the Marines hadn't been a childhood dream, but I certainly liked to play soldier. The lawn mower must have chopped up dozens of those little green plastic soldiers that come in packs of fifty. I admired my grandfather and his service in World War II. I felt honored to go with him to those Pearl Harbor survivor meetings half a century after he served. He used to let me hold the Civil War sword that my great-great-grandfather carried; I only know he was from Iowa and fought for the Union, but he may have been a cavalry officer, based on the sword.

All those things impressed me. But what drove me to enlist was 9/11. That was the catalyst for my military service. I wanted to do something. And so I joined the Reserves and volunteered for the Marine Corps Infantry.

I knew what I might face, although it seemed far more likely to me that I would be deployed to Afghanistan, not Iraq. I remember trying to comfort my mom as she grappled with the fact that her baby boy whom she raised for 18 years was going to go join the infantry.

"Don't worry," I said. "In the Reserves it's just one weekend a month and two weeks a year. And these days, warfare is all technological and it's done from the air." I had a good sense that wasn't the case, but I wanted to comfort her. I know that she was proud of me. But this was her son. She had lived through the Vietnam era—would she see her boy brought home in a box?

She thought about it a while and came back to me with an offer she felt I couldn't refuse. If I let go of this idea of joining the Marines, she said, she would empty her 401(k) retirement plan and buy me a new Corvette. It was my dream car. But I had a bigger dream.

A DEGREE OF INFLUENCE

On the way to that dream, I enrolled at the University of Memphis. I started off as a marketing major, and later, after returning from Iraq, I switched to "political communications," a hybrid of a political science and communications degree.

Though I aspired to be an entrepreneur of some sort, I never felt the path to that was to learn about it in school. I knew from the start that my path wouldn't be to get a business administration degree and then go into business. A degree doesn't guarantee success as an entrepreneur; in fact, many of the profiles I'd read were of people who had been bored with school and dropped out—and later ran highly successful companies.

Many of today's successful entrepreneurs never even went to college. They believed in themselves. They knew they could do it, and persisted. I'm not discouraging college, by any means. Education is valuable. You need to be intellectually curious, and the odds of success increase exponentially with education, whether you get a degree or not. The examples of those who succeed without college are not meant to help anyone cop out. They are meant to encourage those who need to find another way.

Though I aspired to be an entrepreneur of some sort, I never felt the path to that was to learn about it in school. Something other than an education is a prerequisite for success – namely, ambition, drive, leadership, creativity.

I recognized that a degree does open doors. I already had a handle on the fundamentals, thanks to all the reading I'd done before going to college. And I was able to test out of all the basic business courses by reading the class textbooks in advance. But the degree validates one's knowledge. For an entrepreneur, it also serves as a safety net in case a business doesn't work out, and I felt it would be reckless not to get one.

Nonetheless, something other than an education is a prerequisite for success—namely, ambition, drive, leadership, and creativity. In my readings, I had seen the traits of those who succeeded and those who failed. I was intent on emulating the positive and steering clear of the negative. One must have a foundation on which to build. Without the right traits, all the knowledge in the world won't lead to success. But with them, knowledge pays dividends.

EXCELLENCE TO EMULATE

My years in the Marines helped me to develop many of the principles and traits that are so central to success. My military service was as crucial to my personal growth as my classroom studies. When I was called up for duty, I had to interrupt my college studies for a while, but I certainly had no interruption in my education.

I eventually got my degree, but it hasn't played a huge role in my success—at least, not in comparison with my Marine service and my experience thus far as an entrepreneur in the real world. I would say the Marines contributed 90 percent and college contributed 10 percent.

Certainly, the Marines were where I honed my ability as a leader. You meet Marines who are such natural leaders that you would follow them anywhere in battle: "Let's move now! We're going to take that machine gun nest, let's go!"—and you do, without question. Other times you lose trust in the leadership. You feel like questioning everything. It's rare, but it happens. But you don't have to go far in the Marines to find plenty of models of excellence to emulate.

The leadership and the life lessons I learned were inestimable. I know I learned far more about psychology from the Marine Corps than I did from my Psych 101 class. I learned real-world applications: how to motivate, how to discipline, and how people respond differently. When you see how you and others perform under stress, and what works and doesn't work, you have gained something that you cannot gain from a textbook. Books have long played a big role in my life—but not the biggest.

CHAPTER 3:

· ·

FAILURE BEGETS SUCCESS

Things had been tough for quite some time—and when I answered the phone one day, I knew that an entrepreneurial dream had died. I had 72 hours to report to infantry squad leader school at Camp Lejeune, North Carolina. I was being called back to Iraq for a second tour.

It was 2007, and I had been busy trying to make it as an entrepreneur. I was hoping to ride the tide the way so many people were trying to do before the economic collapse. I was intrigued by those TV shows where people were making a killing by flipping houses. Lots of people were doing it, and I wanted to cash in. The opportunity seemed huge, and so I had started Baucom Built Construction.

I figured I could flip two or three houses a year and then get into residential and commercial development.

Like so many, I was inside a bubble about to burst. People were investing as unrealistically as those Dutch investors who got caught up in the "tulip mania" of the 1630s—considered the world's first speculative bubble, in which tulip prices rose tremendously (as much as several times a craftsman's annual salary for a single bulb) and then collapsed. I gave my business everything I had, and life had yet to teach me the folly of doing so.

It had started simply. After my tour in Iraq, I used the money I had saved toward the purchase of a house in the Germantown section of Memphis. I didn't want to throw money away on rent. I wanted to gain equity, and I wanted to start early. This was my thinking: If I bought it at age 20, it would be paid off at age 50. I could buy a new place every four years and keep the old ones to rent out at a profit. By the time I reached retirement age, I'd have a strong residual income.

It had four bedrooms, and I was single, only 20 years old, with no kids or any plans to start a family. So I rented my rooms out to fellow Marines and a couple of friends. They paid me $500 a month each, which covered my mortgage, my cable, and my utilities. I figured if I could do this with my own home, why not do it with other properties?

The day I moved into that house, my roommates moved in, too. Renting out the rooms was my plan from the get-go. That way I was actually able to make money by having my own place, rather than struggling to keep up with the mortgage. Anyone can do this, but some people jump on the opportunity and some do not.

Three months after I moved in, the Tennessee Department of Transportation wanted about 10 feet of my property to add a turn lane on the corner. I was expecting to get an offer of perhaps $3,000 or $4,000, some nice pocket change. I got a check for $52,000. I had the house reappraised right away, and the loss of the 10-foot swath had reduced its value by only a few thousand dollars at most. So I netted a $50,000 windfall.

"You're so lucky," I remember my mom telling me, but I don't believe in luck. Sure, I made out on the right-of-way issue, but it was by my own initiative that I managed to buy the house to begin with at age 20, with a good credit score and a down payment. You don't succeed because things just happen to you. I believe you set yourself up for success by getting everything in order so that good things will result. Let's not call that luck. There is certainly "randomness" in business as in life. There's that one great contact you make, relationship you develop, or large vendor that you sign up because you were at the right place at the right time. But the key is that you have to be prepared when presented with an opportunity. Being prepared means that you're already set up for success when that target crosses in front of your scope.

You have to be prepared when presented with an opportunity. Being prepared means that you're already set up for success when that target crosses in front of your scope.

So what would I do with this additional $50,000? I could have bought a car, but all that would have done was to drive up my insurance rate while the car lost value. I wanted to put that windfall to work.

I started doing some work on the house, and I quickly saw a business opportunity in gaining equity quickly through upgrades. I started by doing

55

a few projects for others. So many people in those days wanted their house to be painted, or dreamed of hardwood floors and kitchen upgrades. How hard could that be? I could hire the pros to do the work while I ran the business and took care of the sales, which I thoroughly enjoy. I could sell the jobs, and they could do the work. We'd work together, and we'd all win.

Then I bought two houses that needed a full rehab—and that means they needed to be gutted. I had no trouble getting the loans for those two houses. It was easy to get a mortgage in those days, and I had good credit and character. I also got construction loans on top of the mortgages. These were truly fixer-uppers.

MY PERFECT STORM

I could see how the money would be rolling in if things went perfectly. They didn't go perfectly. I was still in college and still in the Reserves—I was trying to run a business under increasingly trying circumstances. I soon was in over my head, and Baucom Built Construction was in trouble. It was like the perfect storm.

Along came the recession. The banks needed higher reserves. The financial storm didn't fully start until the first quarter of '08, but the dark clouds were closing in. One day I got a letter that my line of credit for the construction loans on the houses was being reduced.

Those were tough times all around, which meant homeowners weren't in the mood to pay for much construction work. Not only was I losing my credit, but I was also losing my clients. The phone stopped ringing. And when I did get a call one day, it was the final jeopardy: Nick Baucom was needed in Iraq.

The timing of my entrepreneurial endeavor turned out to be terrible. I was severely overleveraged. I take responsibility for my failures as well as my successes, and I know now that I did not take manageable bites in trying to run that business. I had spread myself thin, hoping to make as much money as I could as fast as I could. This time, unbridled ambition had gotten me into trouble.

I was trying to do everything. In poker-speak, I was "all in"— but the other guys had the better cards. I wasn't focused enough. A customer would ask for a new deck on his house and ask if I also could take down a tree in the yard. "Sure," I'd say, knowing that I could find a guy to do it and make some money for myself. But I didn't stop, whether it was a deck, or a tree, or flooring, or those two dilapidated houses that I was certain I could fix and flip. I was jumping at opportunities and I didn't have a niche.

HOLDING ON TO THE DREAM

Today, with Two Marines Moving, I have my niche. I've learned through experience. No longer am I leveraging everything. I have no investors or loans, other than some truck payments. My company is paying its own way and building itself. The growth is organic, without all those additives.

I no longer owe people money—and that has been a lesson learned. I've been able to repay those to whom I was in debt after Baucom Construction failed. I called up a man to whom I owed about $4,000 for a flooring job and sent him a check. He had long since written it off and forgotten about it, but it's important to set things straight. He deserved his money, and I wanted a clear conscience.

If you're worried about the risks of starting a business, or if your earlier efforts have fallen short, just know that I've been there, and it wasn't very many years ago. I know what it's like to feel financially strapped. I know what it's like to have to tell people you can't fulfill a promise right now because you're out of money. It's gut wrenching. I had trouble getting to sleep, and trouble getting up. I never felt as low in Iraq as I did in those days. But success comes from perseverance and persistence. By taking life's lessons to heart and leaning on experience, you can turn it around. You can build an exciting future.

The only way to lose is to give up. A friend told me about an experience during his Marine Recon Indoctrination. It's a grueling ordeal that, if passed, puts you in a very elite unit. It's nine weeks of little sleep, swimming for hours in the open surf, and miles of running. It takes any Marine to the edge, physically and mentally. The last week was the most stressful, and on the final run the men could see the trucks that would take them back to base—and then were told the exercise would continue two more days. Two of the Marines announced that they'd had enough, that they were done. The instructor asked them to repeat that statement—and then told everyone to get in the trucks, because the course was complete. Everyone passed—except the two who had given up. On a real-life mission, you can't just give up.

If you keep telling yourself that you can't do something, if you keep thinking that success is meant for other people and "that's just not for me," then it's never going to be for you. You can pull yourself up and you can pull yourself out, no matter what your background. I didn't come from a background of privilege. My family budgeted, and we lived day by day. But I was raised with a sense of responsibility, and I was encouraged to dream big. To anyone out there who needs a nudge, let me say the say the same: You can dream big. Just be responsible.

If you keep telling yourself that you can't do something, if you keep

thinking that success is meant for other people and "that's just not

for me," then it's never going to be for you.

RATHER HAVE BEEN IN IRAQ

I hadn't expected to be called for a second tour in Iraq. I knew, of course, that I was eligible since I was still in the Reserves, but Iraq felt like a chapter behind me. It was an experience checked off. I'd done that.

I certainly wanted to deploy, and I did. I felt privileged to be part of the Reservist safety net, but I didn't expect two tours. I'd thought multiple deployments were far more likely for an active duty unit. Donald Rumsfeld had other plans. This was a second full activation, and suddenly my immediate direction was startlingly clear, even as the maelstrom of my business struggles continued to swirl.

We headed out for six months of training. I was at Camp Wilson on the Marine base at Twentynine Palms, California. We were set to deploy to Iraq the next week. It was another hot afternoon near 100 degrees, and we had the weekend off—so why not play football? We got together for a game of five on five. I caught a pass, got tackled— and came up with a broken hand.

I tried to shirk it off at first as no big deal, but I couldn't even hold a weapon. "I just need a couple days of rest," I insisted. "It'll heal up; just give it a little time." It didn't heal. So, I went over to the Navy corpsman, who referred me to our battalion doctor, who referred me to the base hospital, where I got an X-ray.

I was going home to Memphis.

I caught a pass, got tackled – and came up with a broken hand. I tried to shirk it off at first as no big deal, but I couldn't even hold a weapon. I was going home to Memphis.

I spent the duration of my contract recovering from surgery to reset the bones and undergoing physical therapy. I was still on active duty, however. In case of a casualty, I was to be sent as an immediate replacement. As it turned out, our unit took zero casualties during the deployment.

And so my civilian life resumed in Memphis, or as much as it could for a man who knew he could be called to Iraq any day. I had come back to three mortgages and a pile of business debt, with $36,000 a year in sergeant pay. It wasn't a great scenario. I'd rather have been in Iraq.

ONWARD TO WASHINGTON

That attitude changed abruptly in July 2008. That's when I met Christy.

We would still be strangers if she hadn't had trouble putting air in her tires. She was at the counter of a gas station in Nashville, asking for help, when I got in line behind her to pay for my purchase. Four or five others also were waiting in line, so I told the attendant, "You can stay at the counter; I'll go out to help her. I got this."

You could say I knew an opportunity when I saw it.

We went out to dinner, and things grew from there. I was still in the Marines, so she moved temporarily to Memphis to search for suitable employment. Memphis is not known as a mecca of employment opportunity. She did interview with a firm in Memphis that had a fit for her as a corporate recruiter—but the opening was at its Washington, D.C., location. She would be placing accountants for employment in the metro area.

Christy told me her news, and I told her mine.

"I've got a chance at a great job," she said, "but it's almost a thousand miles away. It's in Washington."

"And I'm finally off of active duty," I told her. I'd just gotten my notice.

And so we flew together to the nation's capital. We decided to move there together. Christy had a promising new job. I had little more than a dream.

FAMILIAR TERRITORY

"I'm going to start a business," I told my buddy, Brad, "but what am I going to do?" Brad had been with me in Iraq in 2003, five years earlier. This was Nov. 10, 2008.

I knew there was plenty of money to be made if a business were run properly. I knew I was capable. I knew not to make the same mistakes—I'd already touched the hot stove.

When Christy and I had moved to Washington, we rented a Penske truck, which we packed and unloaded ourselves. It wasn't much fun. Other friends had been asking me to help them move, and though I enjoyed the camaraderie, I felt the sore muscles. Moving can be backbreaking.

And then it struck me: Yes, it's not much fun. And that means it's an opportunity. People don't like to move. They are always looking for reliable help. They have trouble trusting moving companies because they've heard horror stories about rip-offs and bust-ups. I thought about the Marine traits and principles. Many people see Marines as reliable and trustworthy, for good reason. They perceive them as well trained and methodical. To a civilian, that translates to a great work ethic and a solid sense of a responsibility. They see integrity.

"This could be huge," I thought. I loved the marketing prospect, and I also had loved my time in the Corps. I didn't want to reenlist or go the officer route, but I loved working with that military mindset. I enjoyed the company of those who understood what it's all about, who shared our stories of boot camp or Iraq or Afghanistan or wherever duty called. I appreciated the attitude of "let's get it done." I wanted to keep working with Marines.

Today, at Two Marines Moving, we all speak the same language. I know I have a crew of high-quality employees. I know what motivates them. I know what sort of discipline works, and I know what doesn't work. Certainly they are in some ways a breed apart, but I can say this with confidence: I know whom I'm working with.

I also know how and where to keep a close watch. That hadn't been the case in my construction business. I'm honest and expect honesty in others. But in dealing with carpenters and electricians and plumbers, I depended heavily on their integrity. I wouldn't necessarily have known if they had only worked four hours when they claimed it was 16. I could look at the pipes a plumber installed in a house and not have a clue what was involved.

In the moving business, by comparison, it's simple. It's common sense from the start, combined with hard work—and I have a handle on both. I also understand sales, website design, dispatching. I know how to schedule people, having been a Marine platoon sergeant:

"These four PFCs get physicals today, this one gets his wisdom teeth pulled, these 10 need Humvee training, and these three corporals take their exams." It was all about managing people in all kinds of situations, and I was confident in my ability to do that. I knew I needed to do people's jobs better than they did, because then I could hold them to the standard of what I knew excellence truly to be.

THE POWER OF THE BRAND

The Marine image goes a long way toward ensuring confidence in clients. And in some clients, it instills even more. My sales staff asks people about their most pressing concern. Sometimes it's protecting grandmother's antiques. Sometimes it's a timing issue. But sometimes we hear this: "Please make sure you send out Marines who are buff, single, and about 6-foot-2." So that plays into the equation, too. And sometimes it's actually a gray-haired father who would rather his daughter spend time with a known entity if he's paying for her move.

It didn't take long to discover the power of the brand. Five months after I started the company, Christy joined me full time in April as a business partner. The company began growing by leaps and bounds, and she saw the opportunity. At the beginning, I'd call her excitedly, to say: "Hey, I just booked a job for this Thursday, can you believe it?" And soon it was: "I just booked two jobs for Friday, I've got to rent two trucks and hire some help." We quickly went from a few jobs a week, to a job a day, to multiple jobs a day. It wasn't as if we threw this idea against a wall to see what might stick. It was sticking every time. Our trajectory was clear. This wasn't just some sideline. Business was about to boom.

In March 2009, Two Marines Moving was featured on the DailyCandy blog, popular in the metro area particularly among women. At the time, I used my cell phone for all my calls, business and personal. On the day that the feature ran, I got swamped with 100 phone calls, with 100 more requests coming online. The boom had begun.

Christy and I married that March 20. We actually got married impromptu at the courthouse and then came back to work. They say that entrepreneurs marry their jobs. Both of us were truly committed. We had bills to pay and payroll to meet, so we went right back at it. And soon we had a son. As I write this, Isaac is 5 years old.

I have a great business partner in Christy, even though she is now my ex-wife. She's a loyal partner and a friend and a great mom. Living under the same roof wasn't for us, but we're both dedicated to our boy and our business.

LIVING A PASSION

I have come to understand that running a business is in my DNA. Whether it was mowing lawns or hustling sports cards or trying my hand at contracting and flipping houses, I have always looked for ways to make an enterprise flourish. It feels as if I am painting on a blank canvas. Whether I find success or failure, it's my own doing. Two Marines Moving has taken me to a new level, with every day an exciting prospect. That's how it feels to be living a passion—and for me, that's the thrill of being an entrepreneur, of creating something where there was nothing.

I want to be the one to plant a business, to tend it, and to nourish it and grow it. That's the spirit of the entrepreneur, and if you have that within you, you can find whatever expression of that spirit works best for you. If you fail, try again. Don't let people talk you out of a dream, but temper that goal with a dose of realism and always second guess yourself, third guess yourself. But don't do that to the point of giving up. Be confident, and if you question yourself, it just means you are adjusting to make the best decision.

Running a business is in my DNA. Whether it was mowing lawns or hustling sports cards or flipping houses, I have always looked for ways to make an enterprise flourish. It feels as if I am painting on a blank canvas.

As we would say in the Marines, you have to be able to adjust fire. You take your first shot, and then analyze. We don't just unleash the whole battery right away. We observe the impact, and then adjust fire accordingly after seeing where the round landed. We use our map to find our current grid coordinates and then use a compass to plot the azimuth to the target: "Okay, right 200 meters, up 50 meters," you call out over the radio, and then, "Fire for effect." That means drop everything you have. That's when the earth erupts in explosions and the mortar teams rain steel down on the target.

But you don't just start out that way. You've got to get on target first. Once you're there, you do what made you successful again, and again, and again. It's the same in business. It comes down to exhibiting decisiveness, while still taking precautions—so long as those precautions don't paralyze you. You are not lacking confidence when you question yourself. You are showing wisdom. From the outside looking in, a leader might seem to know exactly what to do at every step. But everyone has doubts. They deal with them, and take their best shot.

I have found a business that represents an intersection of my passions. I am a Marine, and I am an entrepreneur—and I want to lead others to a better future.

CHAPTER 4:

. . . .

THE FOG OF WAR

We never knew what might be behind the door. We were in enemy territory, where the unknown could be lying in wait.

Everywhere we went—every government building, every military complex, every former Republican Guard barracks—we had to go in and clear the premises. We didn't stop with the entryway; we cleared every inside door, every corner and angle, every hole in the wall blasted by artillery.

At least a dozen Marines, typically, would crawl through the passageways, although it easily could take an entire platoon to secure a large building, such as a warehouse. First, we would set up inner security, then the outer security, and the assault squad. The inner security keeps guard on all four corners of the building to stop anybody trying to get out. The outer security faces away from the building, looking for any threats in the vicinity where the enemy could be lurking.

And then the assault squad went in. The rules of engagement depended on the situation: Obviously, the scene in Fallujah in 2004 was quite different than what we would experience in a less-hostile city. The assault squad approached the building and got through the door, using a crowbar, battering ram, or whatever it took. We had men specially trained to use explosives. Once the door was breached, the point man would go in first, and then the rest of the fire team would work its way through the building to eliminate any targets within.

We knew we could encounter hostiles at any turn. It was more likely that we'd find a lot of innocent people. The worst situation would be having both. We had to be certain to take the time on the trigger to determine whether any people we encountered were a threat or not. Or did they just happen to be in the wrong place at the wrong time? Maybe they worked in this warehouse. Or were they allies—former Iraqi army members or Iraqi police—who were kidnapped by insurgents? We had a split second to decide whether they meant us harm. The enemy certainly didn't have to ponder the matter: The situation is rather obvious when a Marine in full gear is coming at you through a door.

My unit took fire and we returned fire. Did I ever kill a man? I never had anybody who was five feet in front of me where I pulled the trigger, but we had situations where we spotted someone 200 meters away and I opened fire along with three of my other Marines. Did I find myself in such situations? Yes, absolutely. Was it my bullet? I don't know.

A FINELY TUNED MACHINE

Each of us knew his job. I was a rifleman. We had infantry machine-gunners, typically in groups of two working the outer security. You can't carry one personally, Terminator-style, like Arnold Schwarzenegger. Each squad also had a Navy corpsman who would start triage and attend to anyone injured, whether it was one of our guys or an insurgent.

We were a finely-tuned machine. People have a misconception that the infantry just charges into a building. It's far more nuanced. We operated more like players on a football team. The coach would make the calls, and we each had a clearly articulated position, but we were prepared to cover for anyone else if he went down.

These maneuvers are carefully designed in advance by good minds who analyze each move and what would work best in a given situation. In that way, a military maneuver is basically a business plan. You look to see what is going to work best and follow that plan, without deviating unless you have very good reason. You practice it until it becomes second nature. You limit your exposure, and you keep advancing.

One of the drills that we seemed to practice endlessly in the infantry was leaping and bounding toward the enemy. In the drill, you have a battle buddy with you. When one person is down on the ground firing, providing covering fire, the next is up running five to 10 meters. He then drops and starts firing, as the next person pushes forward 10 meters—and so forth.

It seems simple, but the protocols are strict, and they are set up that way for a reason. An entire platoon or a company or a battalion might be moving forward in that manner, along with supporting fire from mortars, and possibly airstrikes and tanks. That's a lot of moving parts. Usually, we did two or three dry runs on a range, and then a live-fire run. In the dry runs, we'd shout "bang, bang," as if we were 8 years old. But when it came time for the live fire, we appreciated the practice as much as we hated it.

A military maneuver is basically a business plan. You look to see what is going to work best and follow that plan, without deviating unless you have very good reason. You practice it until it becomes second nature. You limit your exposure, and you keep advancing.

We also practiced immediate action drills. Let's say we're walking in a ranger file—one of numerous formations, each for a different purpose—and machine gun fire hits us from the right. Everybody immediately yells "contact right" and drops to the ground, on their stomach. Everyone starts firing. Once fire superiority is established, the squad leaders and fire team leaders then begin to direct their small units straight toward the enemy. The Marines on the left side of the squad stay in place and lay down suppressive fire, increasing their fire rate. The right side then flanks and moves toward the target so that there are overlapping fields of fire. The enemy is usually surprised and overwhelmed by this seemingly illogical response.

This is counterintuitive. The natural instinct for any human in this situation would be to hunker down, stay put, maybe fire back when the opportunity presents itself, and hope for the best. But by going from defense to offense, we seize the initiative. We then make the enemy react to us, much the same as an experienced basketball team controls the pace of the game. In business, too, you often have to think counter-intuitively. While it might feel natural to do X, sometimes you have to get out of your comfort zone and do Y.

"YOU FIGHT LIKE YOU TRAIN"

These maneuvers are not a means to eliminate fear. They are a methodical means of acknowledging the danger and persevering—doing what you must do, regardless of fear. To say that there would be no fear would be a lie. What a Marine must learn to do is overcome it. There's no time for fear. Sure, those emotions creep in beforehand or afterward, but at the moment of the assault there's no time for that. Knowing precisely how to respond in any circumstance is the key to controlling the emotions that can kill you.

By going from defense to offense, we seize the initiative. We then make the enemy react to us, much the same as an experienced basketball team controls the pace of the game. In business, too, you often have to think counter-intuitively.

"You fight like you train." I must have heard that phrase a thousand times throughout my six years in the Marines. It's an ancient concept. The Greek soldier and poet Archilochus offered this take on it: "We do not rise to the level of our expectations. We fall to the level of our training."

We'd be conducting training on a range in 100-degree-plus heat while stationed at Twentynine Palms. It was ridiculously hot, the days were long, and after a couple of weeks of intense training, we were really beat.

And that's when we showed ourselves to be part of the world's finest fighting unit. It was more than physical conditioning. We were mentally conditioned and prepared as well. We saw the heat and our own fatigue as a challenge, an obstacle to overcome. We strove for the next level, as individuals and as a unit. We were pushed to the breaking point, by most people's standards, yet we viewed each drill as if we were truly in combat. Those who went on to the blistering heat of the Middle East knew they could face the real thing. They'd seen it all before.

That's the kind of muscle memory that helped the Navy SEALs go in and take Osama bin Laden in Pakistan. They did a mock-up of the facility, an exact size mock-up of the fences to the compound and exteriors of the buildings, even though they didn't exactly know what the interiors looked like. Then they did a mock-up of the surrounding area—over here, an office, over there, homes. They practiced for six months on that one mission.

When you fight like you train, you know that if X happens, we do Y. If Y happens, we do Z. If Z happens, we go to plan D. There is certainly fast-paced thinking involved, but you don't have time to play out every last detail. You just go back to your training, to your immediate action drills. Some of these things might be seen as slowing down the operation, but they don't do that at all. They're absolutely essential for the ultimate success of the operation.

FORWARD DESPITE FEAR

Fear is a normal human emotion when we face danger, but it's how we respond to that fear that makes a world of difference. If we draw back in confusion and paralysis, then we put ourselves and others at risk. If we take immediate action and confront the danger without delay, then we fend off far greater risks that might lie in wait up ahead.

Marines don't retreat. That's why we never say "repeat" while on the radio. Instead, we say: "Say again your last." Why? If there's static on the radio, "repeat" could sound like "retreat." That's not going to happen. Nor do we use the word "foxhole." Foxes hide. Marines dig in to fight. We call it a fighting hole.

Those "leaping and bounding" drills teach us to face the enemy and eliminate the threat. It sounds counterintuitive—who races toward the sound of gunfire?—but the sooner you deal with a threat, the less chance it has to grow, and the greater your chance to live and prosper.

When you fight like you train, you know that if X happens, we do Y. If Y happens, we do Z. You don't have time to play out every last detail. You just go back to your training, to your immediate action drills.

Those lessons apply as well to entrepreneurs or anyone who hopes to become one. Businesspeople, too, must be prepared to leap and bound as they eliminate the forces that would do them in. They must know the immediate actions to take when a risk arises.

You have to face the threats, and be prepared for them, or you have no chance of overcoming them. If you put too much emphasis on your fears, you're done before you start. There is a "fog of war" in every conflict, a veil of uncertainty. Anyone in business will at some point be looking into the unknown—the fog of business, you might say. One must adjust, improvise, and overcome.

You can have it all figured out, and suddenly your clear business plan isn't working. You can expect some of that—and if you remember the overall mission that you are moving toward, you can adjust fire. You can't expect to know it all yourself. If you think you can, you'll never be able to "move outside the wire," which is Marine-talk for leaving the base.

There is a "fog of war" in every conflict, a veil of uncertainty. Anyone in business will at some point be looking into the unknown – the fog of business, you might say. One must adjust, improvise, and overcome.

On the way to get bin Laden, those Navy SEALs lost a helicopter. They actually had practiced for such a scenario. They also knew how they would handle situations that were far less likely to happen. Losing a chopper was a known unknown, but nonetheless, it was part of the fog that sometimes rolls in. As far as we know, not a single SEAL was lost in that fog.

You can be sure, whether in war or in business, that a time will come for immediate action. You have to go through the drills repeatedly and well in advance so that you don't hesitate at the critical moment. "When I am successful, I will _____," so many people say in the world of business, filling in the blank one way or another. They'll finally start contributing to a retirement plan, or they'll have time to start the morning off right with a daily run, or to attend more networking events, or keep up with the trade journals.

It doesn't work that way. Later isn't the time to do those things. To be the person you want to be, you have to start now. It's the basic training for success. You can't wait for a once in a lifetime opportunity to just drift your way. It's the preparation that gets you to that opportunity. That's what sets the winners apart from the losers.

Marines learn to do what is necessary, without indecision about what might be the best approach. You don't have a bunch of guys debating what to do next. They have clarity because they have prepared for the contingencies. If a helicopter goes down and the engine fails on the Humvee that's supposed to get them out, they still have the confidence that they can hike with a full pack and gear for miles without stopping. A Marine gains confidence from training—from physical and mental preparation. In business, confidence flows from a similar wellspring.

To be the person you want to be, you have to start now. It's the basic training for success. A Marine gains confidence from training – from physical and mental preparation. In business, confidence flows from a similar wellspring.

Careful, deliberate forethought and training are what promote rapid-fire decisions and action in the field. You need to be prepared, thoroughly trained, and ready for anything. When you're under the gun, there's no time to sit and brainstorm about the best way to react. You need to develop the ability to act under pressure.

Entrepreneurship is a lot like that. I believe you should accept a 90 percent solution now rather than a 100 percent solution later. You'll never get to 100 percent. You can get frozen as you ponder what you should do, or what you shouldn't do. You will have so many questions, and you won't have all the answers. Just start taking the first step. Yes, you need to set up your plan and know where you're going, but don't get so caught up in the plan that you fail to execute.

SETTING PRIORITIES

At Two Marines Moving, the lessons and experiences I learned in the military are serving me well at the helm of a booming business. I deal with people issues, and with equipment problems. I troubleshoot, and I take care of the various needs and demands of the customers.

This requires the ability to act quickly and to prioritize. A leader must decide the action that is most important at any particular moment, execute it, and relate it always to the overall mission—and do it again and again and again.

Whether it's a customer issue or an employee issue, or whether it's hiring or marketing or advertising or training, purchasing new trucks or getting a new office, it's a matter of quickly cycling through the options, and choosing the one that's the most valuable. You go 10 yards this time, 5 yards the next, and you filter information constantly as you go.

In battle, if someone gets hit, you have two options: You can focus on the person who was injured, or you can focus on the bigger picture. If Smith takes shrapnel to the leg, do you stop everything to help him? He needs to see a medic as soon as possible, but remember that you're still fighting the enemy. Smith is not top priority. What is a leader to do—take three Marines out of a squad of 10 so that they can talk to Smith and put a bandage on him? That could put the whole squad in jeopardy.

A leader must decide the action that is most important at any particular moment, execute it, and relate it always to the overall mission – and do it again and again and again.

The greater compassion lies in eliminating the most risk. A flesh wound can wait as the group serves the greater good. And what if three or four take a hit? You tend to the most serious cases first. That's war. And that's life. You first deal with the most-pressing matters. That doesn't mean that you don't care about the others, but there's only so much time and so many resources to go around. You have to be able to prioritize.

As a squad leader, my role was command and control of the unit, as if I were one man with 13 trigger fingers and 13 guns. But my job wasn't to pull the trigger myself. I assessed the scenario and made sure each squad member was deployed most effectively. I would be in contact with the command center reporting any firefights. If a helicopter were coming, the pilot certainly needed to know what to expect.

Today, as I lead the squad at Two Marines Moving, I'm not dealing with blood and ordering suppressive fire. But I'm still responsible for assessing the scenario. I identify the business opportunities and the risks and sift through it daily. I prioritize: "Yeah, that's something I could do," I might tell myself, "but my time's not best spent there."

It comes down to choosing the most appropriate course of action to protect your assets—your money, your brand, your business itself. But this is about more than survival. You still want to venture out on patrol to see where you can take new territory—that is, where you can develop clients or expand into a new product line, or whatever the case may be.

You might see two opportunities, both with high rewards. But one is also high-risk, while the other is low-risk. The choice might seem simple, but it takes savvy to identify and evaluate one's options. Every good entrepreneur knows what every good Marine knows full well: You limit your exposure, and you keep advancing.

Most people think a patrol's objective always is to make contact with the enemy, but a recon patrol focuses on gathering information and intelligence. It avoids contact so that the commander can more fully understand a situation before sending in the main force. How many bad guys here? How many machine guns? How many tanks? What's the condition of their equipment? It's similar for an entrepreneur. Without maxing out the credit card or spending your inheritance, how can you test the waters before committing all your resources? Could you consider a joint venture or something on a smaller scale as you gain intelligence?

A business leader must scan the whole terrain. Opportunities and risks can present themselves suddenly, and they often call for rapid-fire decisions. That's when a leader must lean on his training and experience, overcome paralyzing worries, and take immediate action. If several things are happening at the same time, the leader must quickly identify the most urgent matters and do what makes the most sense in keeping with the company's ultimate goals. I felt that way in Iraq. I feel that way at Two Marines Moving.

A business leader must scan the whole terrain. Opportunities and risks can present themselves suddenly, and they often call for rapid-fire decisions. That's when a leader must lean on his training and experience, overcome paralyzing worries, and take immediate action.

A DAY IN THE LIFE

A few years ago I got a call one morning informing me that my senior dispatcher hadn't shown up for work. The crews were waiting around for orders. The man who is currently my chief of training stepped up to take charge. He knew a lot of what to do, but he didn't know all the nuances.

Then, when I got to work and started to deal with that problem, I found that the sales phone was ringing incessantly. A news story about our company had just been published, and I had only about half the staff needed to answer all those calls in a timely manner.

As I tried to make the most of that opportunity, I got a call that a truck had broken down. The crew was stuck and couldn't get to the job. And time was of the essence on that particular job. The customer was depending on us to get it done by 3 p.m. so she could catch a 5 o'clock flight. I soon got the inevitable call from that client: "What's up? I'm waiting. Why isn't the crew here?"

How do you respond on a day like that? Do you cradle your head in your hands and pretend it isn't happening? Or do you tell yourself that this is what you signed up for, and this is the measure of your leadership? I started chipping away and processing. What was the most important matter here? What was possible? Could anything wait?

"Look, I can't get the crew out to you this minute," I told that client. "Their truck broke down. I'll get your job done, one way or another. Let me call you back in 30 minutes."

How do you respond on a day like that? Do you cradle your head in your hands and pretend it isn't happening? Or do you tell yourself that this is what you signed up for, and this is the measure of your leadership?

I took a look at the day's assignments. I saw that a few crews were staffed with four or five people for larger jobs. We rented a U-Haul next door to replace our truck that was down. To staff it, we pulled one person from each of those larger crews. I called the client. "A truck with three movers is on its way and ready to work hard for you." She was impressed by the quick action.

Then I turned my attention to the other pressing matters. The dispatcher finally arrived, highly apologetic. He hadn't set his alarm.

"Look," I said, "I'll run dispatch down here. You go upstairs and help to answer those sales calls." He'd never done sales, but I told him to explain who we were, what we did, and the basics of our pricing. "Tell them this isn't your usual job but that the calls are pouring in because of the news story. Reassure them somebody will call them back within 24 to 48 hours, and get their name, address, moving date, and furniture list."

Later, I would be able to send a text message to each caller, explaining the sudden staffing situation brought about by the good publicity and asking them to bear with us. They understood. In fact, many scheduled their moves right away, out of concern that we'd be fully booked soon. We turned a negative into a positive.

As the day wore on, I learned that the crew on the U-Haul was struggling to keep the pace needed to get that client to the airport on time. I had two other crews that had finished early, so I sent them over free of charge to make up for the fact that we had run late that morning. We ended up with nine people doing that two-bedroom move.

She got to the airport on time. We answered all the sales calls. The truck got fixed. I took care of the dispatching mess. I'd put the people and assets in the right places to make it work. Each of those situations was familiar to me, but until then I hadn't had to face them all in one day. Still, I knew I could encounter such a time as this. It can happen in any business, at any time. I'd been through the drills and knew what to do when the situation called for immediate action. I just shifted into gear. There wasn't time to freak out.

Marines understand the mission but focus on the specific tasks at hand, weighing their relative importance. Solve one problem, and then move to the next, in order of priority. Keep cycling through the issues, going back as necessary to follow up. Find the opportunities amid the challenges. That's the way it is in war, that's the way it is in business, that's the way it is in life.

MINIMIZING THE RISKS

In the Marine Corps, I had to write several of what we called the "five paragraph order." I did those in infantry squad leader school in Camp Lejeune. All officers are required to do them as well.

They're about 40 pages long. In college, students would groan about writing a 10-page paper. This was 40 pages, single spaced, and you only passed with a grade of 90 percent or above. That paper was intricate and detailed, with grid coordinates and administration and supply and logistics, command and control. If it were a business plan, it would cover virtually any contingency.

I've learned clearly that running a business requires me to weigh the benefits against the risks and constantly be deciding which action to take that best serves the bottom line. I remember the days when I didn't do that so well—that is, in my Baucom Built Construction incarnation. There were opportunities in that market, but my timing was dreadful. Sometimes such things are within an entrepreneur's control, and sometimes they are not. That's just the way it is—always has been, always will be.

You can exert considerable influence. I put a lot of weight in the power of leverage. I had read much of what Donald Trump wrote about real estate. He didn't become a billionaire by slowly investing a million and watching it compound at 6 percent. He used the power of leverage. On a $500 million building, he'd take out a massive loan, renovate it into a hotel, and then flip it. I only had my $50,000, but I figured I could put it down as my 10 percent and turn it into $500,000. I learned that leverage works both ways. You can leverage yourself into debt so deep you might despair of ever escaping. I had no safety net to catch me if anything went wrong with my plans.

Running a business requires me to weigh the benefits against the risks and constantly be deciding which action to take that best serves the bottom line.

Two Marines Moving has grown through reinvested profits. I haven't been trying to up the ante on a good growth rate, saying, "Okay, we grew 280 percent over three years, so maybe I could get to 500 percent if I sold a 10 percent equity stake, or if I accepted some high-interest financing so I could expand to a new city." Instead, I have steadfastly taken those manageable bites. I've held tight to my advantage and not diluted it.

When the Marines assault a position, they try to keep a three-to-one advantage. If they are facing 150 of the enemy, the attack force should be 450 strong. That's the safety net. You get increased fire and more opportunities to move elements to work in your favor.

If you get down to one-on-one, you have limited options. Everything must go perfectly. You don't have the leverage you need. You should hold tight to your core, your base—and for an entrepreneur that means your investment of time or money. You have to throw out feelers, as if you were on a recon patrol. The Marines don't send the whole company walking down the riverbank. The commander sends out a squad, tests the waters, sees what's out there, and waits till they radio back. He doesn't risk sending a company of 150 against a battalion of 1,200 Iraqi personnel and tanks. He calls up the chain of command for air support to minimize the risk.

As an entrepreneur, you must study and analyze, but then you must also be decisive. Just remember that not making a decision is a decision as well. You can decide actively that something is just not for you, but if you just sit back passively, then you're letting the situations control you, instead of vice versa. The mission cannot rush forward recklessly, and it must never be mired in doubt. If you step back, it must be a purposeful and tactical retreat that serves your best interest, long term.

The Marines don't send the whole company walking down the riverbank. The commander sends out a squad, tests the waters, sees what's out there, waits till they radio back.

When I bought my second house hoping to flip it, I didn't send out my reconnaissance, so to speak. I didn't test those waters by seeing if that first house flipped successfully. I just went all in for a straight attack, without thinking it through. I basically did it World War I style, when we fought using trench warfare as opposed to maneuver warfare. I got up from the trench, yelled charge, and sent the whole company in the face of hardened machine gun posts and an enemy that was well dug in. Instead, I should have sent out my recon to assess the pitfalls, the perils and the opportunities. I should only have moved forward once I had that new knowledge and new information. Instead, I sent the whole company down the river.

FACING THE UNKNOWN

I think back often to that day in 2003 when I was asked to lead my first patrol in Iraq. I didn't know what to expect. I didn't know whether we would suffer a hit, or whether it would be a walk in the park. But I did what I was called to do.

Most patrols end up with absolutely nothing happening. In hindsight, they were boring, although they didn't seem so at the time since we were constantly braced for the unknown. You never know when you will face danger from the enemy, or even from those rare instances of "blue on blue," or friendly fire. Most patrols are without incident. But there are cases when the whole squad doesn't come home.

I was called to leadership. In a situation like that, you can't just say, "You know what, maybe not. That's not for me." You can't do that. I was eager for the opportunity. If it wasn't going to be me, it was going to be someone else. I understood that it was a great chance to learn, and I was gratified to be chosen for it.

Any hesitation that I felt about leading the patrol was simply because I'd never done it. But everything was in place. I had the ingredients for success. I had the training, and that gave me confidence. I also had the support of my other Marines there. It wasn't me out there by myself.

Sometimes people fail to step forward for fear they will make an ass of themselves. They somehow think everybody's waiting for them to fail. For instance, they may be terrified of public speaking because they believe they will be judged—and yet, it's unlikely that even one person in the audience wants them to do poorly. Likewise, none of my Marines that day was thinking, "I really hope Baucom screws this up."

I knew what was inside me. I had confidence in my training and the support of my brothers—and that's what it takes to show true leadership in facing the unknown. I have carried that confidence forward from my days in the Corps, and it has made all the difference.

THE NATURE OF LEADERSHIP

Effective leadership is about presence and tone of voice. In the Corps, you're taught to stand and speak with authority and take charge of a situation. People naturally are looking for leadership. They want to follow someone they can trust. If you go into a store and, with an air of authority, order everybody outside, a lot of people will go, whether you are wearing a badge or not. Most people find it lot easier just to agree, rather than to come up with their own plan. They will obey a leader whom they can trust.

In return, a good leader takes that trust to heart, using good sense and showing responsibility. A leader finds and keeps followers by becoming a calming influence, whether in the heat of battle or the thick of business. It's important to remain unflappable, even as others panic. You cannot shrink from the occasion. Those whom you are leading will need to know what is going on and what they are supposed to do next, and you must be there for them. Bravery is infectious, just as cowardice is infectious.

I confess that sometimes I didn't know what was going on, but a leader must start with projecting authority until he figures it out, and then move forward to get it done. It's best not to fake it, of course, but you do need to instill confidence in others. If you act decisively, even amid uncertainty, that confidence will develop quickly.

A leader is simply performing a vital function—as are those whom he or she directs. We all look to others for direction. Leaders have their own leaders. We all play multiple roles: You might be a follower in one realm of your life and a leader in another. In a company, employees need a CEO who will direct the big picture so that they can do their jobs effectively. The CEO needs employees who will fulfill the company's objectives. And all along the rank and file are supervisors and superiors of various stripes to whom others report, and who report to others.

Bravery is infectious, just as cowardice is infectious. A leader needs to instill confidence in others. If you act decisively, even amid uncertainty, that confidence will develop quickly.

A TIME TO JUST FIRE

Let's say I'm 500 yards from a target, an enemy bunker. I've got clear vision on the bunker. I can see that there's an enemy in there.

My first thought might be this: "Why would I put my Marines in jeopardy when I could just call in mortars? They're extremely effective, and there's a mortar position just two miles behind us."

And then my second thought might be: "They can't see the target from there, though. The GPS might be off because of that ridge over there, and I certainly don't want them to drop a mortar on our own unit."

And my third thought, as I look at the target: "Are they going to see me first? What if they attack while I'm trying to figure this out?"

You could analyze this decision for a long time. That's not leadership. The best approach might be to drop mortars that purposely fall short, then adjust based on where they hit, moving progressively closer. That way you are taking action while continuing to analyze the situation—if you have time for that.

It's a strategy that applies to business as well as to warfare. Advance preparation and careful thought are indeed important. Impetuous behavior can lead to trouble. You must assess risk, but don't expect to eliminate it. There comes a time for action and decision, and you might need to make those decisions on the spot, trusting in yourself and in everything that's gotten you to this point.

In other words, you can't sit in meetings and ponder the problems and wait forever. In military terms, there's a time when you "just pull the trigger."

I grow frustrated with any office meeting that lasts longer than about 15 minutes. I tend to get up and get on with the tasks of the day. If you can't come to a conclusion in 15 minutes that means you're just talking about it. It's time for action. Let's get to the heart of the matter, and then let's move.

You can't sit in meetings and ponder the problems and wait forever. In military terms, there's a time when you "just pull the trigger."

We can sit here and spend eight hours talking about it, or we can spend 15 minutes talking about it and seven hours and 45 minutes acting on that. Guess which one's going to produce the best results?

CHAPTER 5:

·· ·

FINDING YOURSELF, SELLING YOURSELF

I'm considering joining the Marines," I told the recruiter, "but I've also been talking to the Army. I like their bonus. Do you think you could match it?"

The recruiter peered at me. "It sounds like you're asking me why you should join the Marine Corps."

"Well, yes," I said. "I mean, the Army has this $5,000 bonus that—"

"—I've got a question for you," he said, cutting me short. "What I want to know is why I should *let you* join *my* Marine Corps."

That's what sold me—that attitude, that confidence. Sure, that $5,000 would have been a lot of money for an 18-year-old, but the recruiter basically said, "Screw your $5,000 bonus. What makes you think you're worthy of joining us?"

"I've got a question for you," the recruiter said, cutting me short. "What I want to know is why I should let you join my Marine Corps."

Whether he recognized something about me that made him change his tactics or he just used the pitch every time, it worked perfectly. I stopped thinking about bonuses because I knew that he had the superior product. My next thought was, "Sign me up!"

Years later, in 2004, I spent six months as a Marine recruiter in Memphis. Recruiters were usually higher-ranking staff non-commissioned officers, so I knew I had to sell them on taking me as a lance corporal. They initially said, "Thanks, but no thanks." To them, I was just a young guy who was going to require training and might not even work out. I was an inconvenience they didn't want to shoulder.

I thanked them for their time, but I was far from finished. I went right home and typed up a two-page letter to show them exactly how *they* would benefit. I was in school at the University of Memphis at the time, so I wrote that I would be their go-to guy on the inside that could talk directly to 20,000 eligible students. I would wear my uniform every day and answer questions. I knew the audience because I essentially *was* their audience. If they had to recruit two Marines a month, I'd get them one.

And it worked. I wasn't the right rank and I didn't go to school for the proper recruitment training, but I made my numbers every month.

I volunteered for recruiting duty for a couple of reasons. I knew it would help me to get a promotion, for one. For each person that you recruit, you get points toward your promotion. And I wanted the experience. I like sales. I like talking with people. I also was passionate about the cause and mission. I believed the Marine Corps would help a lot of people move forward and progress in their lives. It wasn't like I was selling Ginsu knives.

Recruiting duty was a temporary assignment. It was a three-month contract that my recruiters extended an extra three because of my performance. I met my target goals, made my seniors' jobs easier, and learned a lot in the process. Upon the completion of my contract, I elected to leave the recruiting office to focus on school.

I learned so much about sales and people in those six months that I still use today at Two Marines Moving. Sales and marketing are critical. Whether your business is manufacturing, construction, professional services, or contracting, you have to get the sale if you are going to succeed.

The first thing I learned was how to deal with "no." As a recruiter, I was often handed a list of names and numbers to contact graduating seniors in high school who had submitted requests for information on USMC.com. At first, it was brutal. We were asking these kids to devote four years of their lives to the Marines, and I definitely heard "no" far more often than "yes." But I came to realize that you have to get through all of those nos to get to a single yes. It became a numbers game. If I knew it would take 99 nos to get to the one yes, then I just started to say, "Bring on those 99 people, because I want that yes."

I also learned a lot about the psychology of dealing with people, about what motivates people, and the various reasons that people come to the same table. They come from such diverse backgrounds, yet they're all in the same place looking for something. They're in search of something better. Different people respond to different things, and I figured out what was important to each person as an incentive for joining the Marines. Was it travel? Was it patriotism? Was it family heritage? Then I would speak to the point that was most important to that individual. There might be 15 main reasons to join the Marine Corps, but this prospective recruit didn't care about reasons four through 15. He cares about reasons one through three, so I didn't even waste my time on those other reasons. Instead, I prioritized and talked about those three that interested him.

If people just walked in to the recruiting office, I'd try to engage them and strike up a conversation to find out why they were interested. There's a whole process behind joining. It's not as if this were 1776 and we had to get the militia together and grab our muskets and head right out to battle. We would go through a checklist of medical history, psych history, and education level. They'd go through testing and a full physical.

We'd see what jobs were available and try to find a match. Not everybody comes in and says, "I want to be infantry." Many say, "I'll be anything but infantry." Maybe they have a particular background or interest. Maybe they're fascinated by computers and programming, which would put them in the cyber-warfare MOS, which stands for "Military Occupational Specialty." That's military jargon for "job."

We also made sure the recruits were prepared physically for boot camp. We don't just put people on a bus or plane and drop them in boot camp and hope everything works out. As recruiters, it was our responsibility to send people who were prepared. They're certainly going to be in great shape when they come out of boot camp, but they have to go in at a base level.

The most important thing that I learned is that you can have the greatest product on Earth, or the most remarkable service, but if nobody is paying for what you offer, it doesn't matter. You need to get the word out. People need to know you exist, and they need to have a reason to deal with you. They need to understand clearly what you can do for them, and how you can do it better than anyone else. That's what marketing is all about, and that's the role I played as a Marine Corps recruiter. Your efforts must lead to the sale, or what's the point? It's an extremely important part of the equation for business success.

"KNOW THYSELF"

Much more recently, I have been involved in the transition assistance program—which you could say is on the other end from the recruiting side, because it serves Marines who are getting out of the service. The transition assistance program is a course of about two weeks on such skills as resume writing and networking. I go to Marine Corps bases in the D.C. area.

In the program, I talk to them as an employer, a couple times each month—in groups as small as a few dozen and as large as a couple hundred. We discuss their next moves and how to pursue job opportunities. I urge them not to forget what they learned in the Corps.

"I know it was drilled into you," I tell them, "and you probably don't want to hear 'attention to detail' or 'adapt, improvise, and overcome' ever again. But remember that stuff whether you're deployed to Afghanistan or you're trying to get a job—or start a business. The tools you learned to use for combat will serve you well in your career. It's up to you to use them."

These are people who are ready to make the adjustment to civilian life. The big question is "so what's next? Where do I go from here?" I intend to continue my involvement in the TAP program. Not only is it an opportunity to show others how they can thrive in civilian life, but it also is a recruiting opportunity for my business.

I always ask whether anybody in the room wants to start a business. Usually out of about 40, a few raise their hands. I tell them to talk to me afterward, because I'm not going to speak to the entire audience on that if only a couple people are interested. Although the military produces more self-starting entrepreneurs than the public at large, most still are focused on finding a job with a wage.

Later, when I talk to those few who aspire to business, they usually ask me what's the most important thing they need to know, or how I would handle a situation, or what I think about an idea they have. I tell them to add me on LinkedIn, so they've got a resource there. Those who have started or want to start a business are the ones with whom I communicate most easily. I know so well what it's like.

These men and women are still searching—just as they were when they joined the service. They still are on a quest to better themselves, but now they are looking to move on from the Marine Corps. Most of them thoroughly enjoyed their time there. The good times and even the bad times will all become fond memories. Their service was life changing, but they are ready for what's next. They're ready for school. Or they have their degree and they're ready for a new career.

What they might be lacking is an understanding of just who they are. We're all on that journey, to a greater or lesser extent, for all of our lives. "Know thyself," the ancient Greek philosophers advised. We're all trying to understand why we are here and what we have to offer.

I find that veterans often are searching for their niche. It can take awhile to discover it. Some only have a vague sense of what motivates them to get up in the morning. They have yet to learn what truly interests them. I can give advice on writing resumes and networking, but beyond that, each of us needs to come to understand what motivates us, what excites us in life.

POWER OF PERSISTENCE

I can show my fellow Marines how persistence and tenacity and follow-through will pay off. A Marine learns in boot camp how to keep at it, but that's a quality that must continue for years thereafter—in the service, and out.

You will have setbacks, be it at boot camp or in business. It's a matter of getting back up and always pressing onward, without getting discouraged. Don't retreat.

You might take an "operational pause," as we did in 2003 on the push to Baghdad. We were a few weeks into it, and about 150 miles from Baghdad. Massive sandstorms had slowed our supply lines of food and water, ammunition, and other supplies to the frontline troops. Iraqi sandstorms are something to behold. I got lost in one once on the way back from the latrine. I had to use night-vision goggles to see the path under my feet. This wasn't Memphis anymore.

The sandstorms forced an operational pause, where we stopped, took account of where we were and where we wanted to go, and realigned and adjusted things.

You will have setbacks, be it at boot camp or in business. It's a matter of getting back up and always pressing onward, without getting discouraged. Don't retreat.

You won't always be gaining ground in any endeavor. There will be times when you need to pause and reflect before pushing forward again. As long as it's just an operational pause, you're fine. As long as you don't lose your momentum, you will come out stronger than ever. That the power of persistence.

"How do I get a job?" veterans often ask me. The answer: Be persistent. Or they ask: "How can I get a business started?" Be persistent. "How am I going to make something of myself?" Be persistent.

It's an absolute requirement. If you lack that quality, you will fail. There is no way around it. It's an ironclad law: You have to have persistence to get anything done of any meaning.

"How do I get a job?" veterans often ask me. The answer: Be persistent. Or they ask: "How can I get a business started?" Be persistent. "How am I going to make something of myself?" Be persistent.

ONE FOOT IN FRONT OF THE OTHER

In boot camp, you get used to a routine that is anything *but* routine. You don't know what's going to happen from one moment to the next. The drill instructors know. But from the recruits' perspective, it's three months of having no idea what they will face. They hear rumors, perhaps, from someone who got a copy of the training schedule, that this will be rifle qualification week, or that they will be doing swim qualifications. But then, seemingly out of nowhere, it's this: "All right, everybody up for a five mile run."

Boot camp is physically and mentally demanding. The average workday at boot camp is 16 hours. It's as far from a 9-to-5 routine as you can get. Some recruits don't make it. Out of my platoon of about 100, five or six couldn't hack it. One tried to get out by ingesting a lot of salt, hoping to raise his blood pressure for the medical screening. I don't know if that worked. I do know that one day he was in our platoon and the next day he wasn't.

Most recruits are fresh out of high school. If they were five minutes late to homeroom several times, they might have had to stay after class. No big deal. Now, it seems they need to be 15 minutes early for everything. If they don't show, it's called a UA, unauthorized absence. Very big deal.

I learned to think positively. I remember another recruit's comment: "They can't stop time." Despite all the rigors and the tough treatment, we knew the exact day of graduation. It was October 11, a date I still remember because I looked forward to it so much. It was the day when I would be done with boot camp and become a Marine.

Meanwhile, we would find ourselves waking up at 3 a.m. for a five-hour hike covering 20 miles at a brisk pace, carrying 100 pounds of gear. It's one foot in front of the other, measuring the miles and measuring the days. Time marches onward, too, and the day will come when you are done.

You can stay positive by remembering that big picture. "This might be miserable now," I told myself, "but the rewards are coming, and I'm going to earn that title." It truly is one to be earned. When you look back at those days, you are proud of what you did. Those were your first steps toward finding yourself.

A PERSPECTIVE OF RESPECT

Drill instructors yell. No surprise there. But young recruits might be surprised at how deeply they usually come to respect that instructor, despite the harsh treatment.

On those long hikes, who was up front every time? It was the drill instructor, right there with us, leading us. He was proving that he wasn't asking us to do anything that he hadn't done himself. He was demonstrating that he was willing to do it, again and again.

Sure, the drill instructor can come up with some creative punishments—sometimes comical ones. It's pretty funny looking back, and it's also pretty funny when it happens to someone else in your platoon. It's just not funny when it happens to you.

But these guys are no monsters. You come to see that they are dedicated leaders who have your best interest in mind. They all go home to their families or their girlfriends. I'm sure there were Marines under my command who muttered, "That Sgt. Baucom is such a hard ass." But all they knew was that my first name was Sergeant and my last name was Baucom. They knew nothing of my personal life, but I had their respect without a doubt.

It's a matter of perspective. I remember the humps I did with my unit at Camp Pendleton. Arduous? Yes. Monotonous? Yes. Physically demanding? Of course. But I knew I would be getting off for the weekend to hang out with my friends on Mission Beach or over at La Jolla. I thought about those Marines who endured far longer hikes—hundreds of miles on the battlefronts of Europe and Asia and wherever they were called. I thought of the men at the Battle of Chosin Reservoir in Korea, the "Frozen Chosin," who marched into an onslaught of Chinese mortars at 30 degrees below zero. And there I was in sunny California waiting for my weekend.

So much depends on how you look at things. When you consider what others have had to face, you feel a little less sorry for yourself and a little more respectful of those who paved your way. You certainly don't take it personally if a drill instructor—or the boss—gets in your face. You come to see what he's trying to do for you. He's seen it all, and when you, too, can see that big picture, you're willing and able to march on.

I thought of the men at the Battle of Chosin Reservoir in Korea, the "Frozen Chosin" who marched into an onslaught of Chinese mortars at 30 degrees below zero. And there I was in sunny California waiting for my weekend.

FINDING A JOB IS A JOB

Sometimes people have a perception that, "All right. I'm getting out of the military, so I just need to upload my resume on Monster. com and let's see what happens." It's wishful thinking, at best, and getting a job that way will take a long time, if you get one at all.

Completing your resume is the base level, but then how do you build on that? Do you just copy and paste that one document and post it here and there? If you establish a presence on a variety of online career sites—and there are many of them—you have made a start, but it doesn't stop there. You need to tailor that resume to each company. Whenever I get a resume that says, "My objective is to obtain a job at Two Marines Moving," I know this is not some generic resume that was sent to me and 300 other companies.

Think of finding a job as being a job in itself. If you put 40 hours a week into getting a job, you'll have one a lot quicker than if you just apply on one job board and sit at home waiting for that phone call.

You should get out to career fairs and networking events. I go to Marine Corps Business Owners and Executives Association meetings. For anybody looking to start a business, that's a good peer group to be around. You're surrounded by Marines who are founders, presidents, vice presidents, owners of companies, chief marketing officers, etc.

Think of finding a job as being a job in itself. If you put 40 hours a week into getting a job, you'll have one a lot quicker than if you just sit at home waiting for that phone call.

I notice people's attitudes when they come in for an interview. At Two Marines Moving, they often come to the office in a polo shirt and jeans or khakis. That's acceptable. But you can bet that I notice when an applicant arrives in suit and tie. He's not communicating, "This is just a moving job." After my recruiter finishes the interview, I'll immediately be asking him, "Who was that guy? What's his name? What's his rank? Does he have any leadership abilities? Could he be promoted to dispatching in short order? Could he be promoted to sales?" Just by his dress, the man has stood out from the pack. He made a good impression. If he had dressed like a slob, he would have signaled that he wasn't serious.

You build on that impression by sending out those thank-you cards after the interview, and you just keep at it. You don't easily take no for an answer—because, as I learned, you'll encounter "no" plenty of times on the way to a "yes." You make follow-up calls. You do everything you can to make sure that you're top of mind.

Back when I applied to become a Marine recruiter after returning from Iraq, I was turned down at first. "It's not in the budget," I was told, which is a nice way of saying no. I followed up with a letter to the head recruiter there. I probably wrote a couple pages. I knew that I not only would be helping others but also that I would be helping myself get a promotion. It was a combination of selfless interest and self-interest—and that is also the case today as I help veterans in the TAP program while also scouting for potential employees.

In that letter, I did my best to sell myself. I explained who I was and how my background would help them. I pointed out that I would be on campus every day, where the 20,000 students who go to the University of Memphis would be able to see me in uniform, which I would wear to class every day. I told them that I would talk to people randomly in the cafeteria about the Marines. I was part of their target population, I explained, and could help them fulfill their mission every month.

I marketed myself to get that job. I asked myself how I was going to appeal to that head recruiter. I knew he had his quota to make every month, and so I showed him how I could help meet that need. And, in turn, once I had the job, I learned that recruiting had a lot to do with marketing and sales. Whether I was doing presentations at high schools, or cold-calling students from the office, or working with potential recruits who walked through the doorway, I was honing my skills. I was selling people on why they should sign over four years of their life to the Marines. Any other sales job would seem easy by comparison.

I always kept sight of the fact that I was dealing with flesh-and-blood human beings who were grappling with their career paths and their futures. Recruiting is a job that calls for caring and compassion. That's true salesmanship—when you are showing people something that could better their lives and helping them decide whether it's for them. When you recruit for the Marines, or for a company, you are looking out for the organization's best interests, certainly, but you are dealing with people who have families and aspirations, and need you to serve their interests.

I would say about 10 percent of those who walked into the office knew they wanted to be a Marine and just wanted to know where to sign. The rest weren't sure. Some had just seen a commercial and knew little more than that about the Corps. Some happened to be passing the recruiting office and stopped in on impulse to check it out. It was up to me to connect the dots on why they were there and how we might best serve them.

Recruiting is a job that calls for caring and compassion. That's true salesmanship – when you are showing people something that could better their lives and helping them decide whether it's for them.

If getting an education seemed to be the main goal, I could tell them all about the GI Bill, which fully pays for college plus a monthly stipend. Or maybe the potential recruit had a kid on the way and no health insurance. I could tell him, "Here's a job with health insurance and a pension after 20 years." That's also the message for the career-minded. And some would come in and more or less say, "I want to shoot guns and blow things up," in which case I talked about the travel and adventure.

The recruiter must tailor the message. It's a marketing and sales job that helps people find and fulfill their purpose in life and what would be suitable for them. The recruiter is looking for a good fit. You shouldn't join the Marines just for the sake of being in the Marines. The Corps is the smallest branch. It is like a family. I was in boot camp with people I later met again in Iraq or at Camp Pendleton. Because it's like a family, you feel accountable: You want to see your Marines do well—and you don't want to usher someone into the family who just doesn't belong.

WHERE PASSION AND PURPOSE INTERSECT

Today, as I run my business, I am called upon daily to use my leadership skills. I am putting that ability to good use in a profitable venture, whether it came to me by nature or by nurture. Leadership may be in my blood, or it may have come to me through my military and life experience. Both played a role, I believe.

With Two Marines Moving, I get to do the marketing of my own company. I get to continue to refine my leadership skills. I get to give veterans jobs and provide them assistance. Some, I know, are with me only for a time, as they transition. A lot of people in the D.C. area are working on contracts. They might have a nine-month contract on a project, and as soon as it's over, they're laid off. So they come back here and they work here for two or three more months until they pick up another contract. My company, in a way, is their safety net.

Two of my former employees have gone on to start their own businesses, and both have been successful. I've seen people grow from entry-level mover to team leader driver to crew chief and then over into sales, while working on a degree. Civilian recruiters take note of such ambition. They see the promotions, and they want such people on their own team.

I run a moving company that's on the move—and I am helping people, whether employees or clients, who are moving on and moving up. I am still a recruiter. I am helping people to grow, to serve their own families, and to move forward in life. I now have about 100 employees. I can see the day when I will have 1,000. Each is an individual with dreams and hopes and goals. Like the drill instructor leading the march, I want to be right there with them to show that I, too, have done, and am still doing, the tasks they face.

Many of these people are, in effect, getting their basic training for life. I get to work with them. And I get to run a profitable business. I get to be a Marine and an entrepreneur. I have found the intersection of passion and purpose in my life.

I hope that by sharing my own story—and how I discovered my own niche—that I can inspire others to success. They know that I'm one of them. Though I no longer am in the Reserves, I am still a Marine. It's a calling. It may sound like a cliché, but it's very true. When you become part of the Corps, it becomes part of you for a lifetime.

★ ★ ★ ★ ★ ★

I run a moving company that's on the move – and I am helping people, whether employees or clients, who are moving on and moving up. I am still a recruiter. I am helping people to grow, to serve their own families, and to move forward in life.

★ ★ ★ ★ ★ ★

CONTINUOUS IMPROVEMENT

The Japanese have a business philosophy called *kaizen*, which emphasizes the importance of continually improving—every day, slightly better, ever upward. By improving practices and efficiency, in myriad small ways, they do wonders for the bottom line and the reputation of their industries.

It's a great business philosophy, and it's a great philosophy for living. We all need to work to constantly improve our situation. Certainly, it's good to have that big crazy goal, but to get there you have to tweak. You could spend a lot of time and resources figuring out some big move that will grow your company 100 percent. Instead, you could make 10 small decisions that each improve the company by 10 percent, and you've reached that goal.

I'm a little over six years in business now, and not a day goes by when we don't tweak something. For example, we now put our logo on all our packing boxes. That way, if the box sits in someone's basement for 10 years, it becomes free marketing for us.

Small matters such as that can add up to significant improvement for a business. You can start to make such small changes in your life, too. As we tweak ourselves to improve day by day, and as we learn more about ourselves, we become better people, both on the job and off.

"NICK, IT NEVER ENDS"

One day, when I had been in business about three years, I was talking to my mentor, Oscar Wiygul. I was already doing about $2 million a year in revenue. I'd had a long day at the end of a long week. "Oscar, when does this end?" I asked him. I felt I'd seen enough success to deserve a break.

"Nick, it never ends," he told me. "It never ends. You're always going to be modifying and adjusting and managing. It's never going to manage itself. If it did, then everybody would do it."

Oscar is not only a mentor but also a very good friend who has contributed greatly to my success. I met him about four months after I started the business. He owns a chain of car repair shops, and his location near me has a U-Haul franchise. I needed some blankets for a move.

He saw by the license plates on my car that I was from Memphis. He had moved to Washington from Memphis decades earlier. We started talking about our town and got nostalgic about barbecue, and then I told him about my company. He welcomed me with open arms. He offered to clear a room in his business so that I could have office space—at that point, I still was meeting up in a parking lot with my crews. About a month later, I took him up on the offer. I went out to dinner with him a couple times, and he had Christy and me over to his house for dinner with his family.

Today, I think of him as the chairman of my board. He's not officially on our board, but any time I've had an issue or a problem, it's stuff he's seen before. He's been able to offer expert guidance.

That resource has been extremely important. Five years ago I hadn't been through a lot of the trial and tribulations of owning a business yet. When I faced those, he was able to give some great advice based on his background, intelligence, and experiences. Today, he would refer to me as a peer. I still have much I can learn from him, but it's interesting how this relationship has developed: He learns a lot from me now, too.

His mentorship developed through friendship— a couple of guys just chatting about what works and what doesn't work. Anyone who wants to be an entrepreneur should reach out to others who have been there.

Leaders can feel lonely there at the top. You need someone to give you perspective. A mentor can help you avoid the mistakes that he or she made in the past. Experience matters. It's like the difference between a green 18-year-old who has been in combat for a week and a salty sergeant on his fifth tour, emanating confidence. Oscar made it clear to me how much I needed to be open to mentoring. I felt confident, maybe even borderline cocky, but I wasn't a know-it-all. I hung on to every word he said because I respected him and his wisdom and the time he spent with me. He told me later that he was impressed with how I had handled his advice and suggestions. I didn't always agree with him, but I always humbled myself and kept an open mind.

Oscar's primary message to me when we met had been, in effect, "Hey, it doesn't end; you always need to keep at it, to be persistent." He was telling me that if I wanted growth, I couldn't rest on my laurels. I needed to get my ass back to work. I needed to take action. Oscar was never in the military, but he would have made a great

Marine. He has helped me keep in touch with the man I know myself to be.

Leaders can feel lonely there at the top. You need someone to give you perspective. A mentor can help you avoid the mistakes that he or she made in the past. Experience matters.

CHAPTER 6:

· ·

TAKING CARE
OF OUR OWN

I was passionate about politics and how the world works even before I knew much about either. I gleaned what I could from books when I was a teenager, but my tour in Iraq opened my eyes to the wider picture. Later, back home, I kept asking myself how my small role as a lance corporal fit into the greater meaning of it all. In other words: Why had I gone to war? Where did I fit in?

That's why, back in Memphis, I switched to "political communications" as my major. The "political" part was in keeping with my keen interest in everything from global climate change to the international monetary fund to state and local politics. The "communications" part was in keeping with my predilection for public speaking. One of my favorite classes at the university was argumentation and debate. I enjoyed its interactive nature and the opportunity to learn from others and prepare a case.

I had a desire to learn new things. I chose to write a paper on the Falklands War simply because it was one conflict that I had yet to understand. I wanted to explore new territory, not revisit the old. That's the point of education.

I once aspired to be congressman or a senator, and that also had a lot to do with why I chose that specific degree. I wanted to be well versed in our political system, and I wanted to communicate effectively. The degree seemed tailored for me. No longer do I have a desire to run for public office, but I have never lost my desire to learn where I fit into the bigger picture. One cannot isolate oneself from the political landscape—and I certainly wanted to further explore that question of why people go to war, and whether they should or should not.

As I considered different careers, I knew this much about myself: I was a leader at heart. As I evolved in learning about myself and the world, I realized I wanted to help others to develop and grow by operating a business of my own.

That has come to pass. I want to tell others the same things that my mentor Oscar talked to me about, those real-life business principles that you cannot learn from a textbook. No matter how good your grade on an exam, you cannot embrace those principles until you have lived them.

As I have watched my own employees catch the entrepreneurial bug and launch businesses, I know that what they learned at Two Marines Moving will serve them well. As a businessman, I can directly see how I have influenced an individual's path to success. To me, that is far more satisfying than giving a political stump speech to raise campaign funds.

As I evolved in learning about myself and the world, I wanted to help others to develop and grow by operating a business of my own.. I want to tell others the same things that my mentor Oscar talked to me about, those real-life business principles that you cannot learn from a textbook.

A BROADENING VIEW

When I went to Iraq amid the post-9/11 backlash against terrorism, I felt fully in favor of our intervention there. The Marine Corps is a pretty homogeneous group. You wouldn't have found many Marines who thought we shouldn't have been in Iraq.

Over time, though, one begins to wonder. As I began asking myself why we were there, and as I researched and pondered the matter, my worldview widened. I doubted the wisdom of the US invasion. I have come to see the interconnectedness of humanity. We're a global village, not isolated pockets. We need to carefully consider those connections and not take things at face value.

We can't ignore one another—either interpersonally or internationally. We're here to serve one another, making the most of our own strengths and the strengths of those around us. That's an important lesson for leaders, whether they are diplomats, businesspeople, or heads of a household.

We can't ignore one another – either interpersonally or internationally. We're here to serve one another, making the most of our own strengths and the strengths of those around us. That's an important lesson for leaders, whether they are diplomats, businesspeople, or heads of a household.

THE POWER OF DELEGATION

When I started Two Marines Moving, I was the salesman, the dispatcher, and the mover. I was all of the above. I was the chief imagination officer and the creative person, and I was the one who answered the phone to book the job, and then picked up the furniture and put it down.

That worked at first, but my business has grown. I couldn't possibly serve all those roles today. A leader must focus on leading, while delegating jobs to others—including those tasks at which others have greater expertise. As the leader of a business, my focus must be on managing others.

Yes, leaders must inspire and encourage their followers, but in the day-to-day operations of a business, they must tell them what to do and hold them accountable for getting the job done—and done well. As Oscar reminded me, it never ends. A leader must be the keeper of goals and the manager of results, and must also be the dispenser of discipline and appreciation. A leader must continually attend to those duties.

On my staff today, I have a sales manager. I have an operations manager, and a senior dispatcher. Each of those people has staffs of their own. Then I have the people in the field—the movers, the muscle. We use job titles that relate to my Marine experience with ranks. My entry-level employee is called a crew member, which in the Marine Corps would be an E3 or below—a private, private first-class, or a lance corporal. The next level of seniority is the team leader, who is like a corporal and is in charge of the moves and interacting with the client. Team leaders manage their subordinates during the move, whether it's one other person or three others.

The next level up is crew chief, who is like a sergeant. If we have a larger job with a lot of moving parts, requiring 10 or 15 people for a full workday, then my crew chiefs are in charge. There are fewer crew chiefs, of course, than team leaders, and fewer team leaders than crew members.

My dispatchers are like platoon sergeants. If I have 40 people heading out—about the size of a Marine platoon—the dispatchers are in charge of logistics and support so those workers get out the door properly, fully uniformed, with a positive attitude, knowing their mission for that day. The dispatchers make sure they have the right number of blankets and enough fuel in the truck. The dispatchers also interact with the clients to make sure the people on site are doing the job as expected.

Meanwhile, my four-person sales staff is responsible for dealing with clients on the phone. If it's a larger job, they're going out to meet that client in person and represent our brand from the first handshake.

THE RIGHT PEOPLE IN THE RIGHT POSITIONS

In the hierarchy at Two Marines Moving, each job requires people with the right qualifications, whether it's muscle or people skills. We can see during the job interview how a candidate would likely fit in best with us, if at all.

It's similar to the Marine assessment and evaluation, although that's more formal and on a much larger scale. In the aptitude testing, one applicant might be suited for military intelligence, another for communications. Another might be a born mechanic. All recruits know from the get-go which job they are slated to do. The testing reveals the recruit's capability, and the recruit expresses a preference. When there's a good fit, the new Marine is buying into the process from the start.

At Two Marines Moving, each job requires people with the right qualifications, whether it's muscle or people skills. We can see during the job interview how a candidate would likely fit in best with us, if at all.

My company is small enough that I can see the range of skills and how people interact. We promote from within about 95 percent of the time. Before a promotion, we are able to see how a crewmember handles a move, and handles himself, over and over again, and we see what skills he possesses beyond muscle power. Let's say a mover shows he is personable with clients. In addition, his paperwork is thorough and reliable—no credit card errors, all waivers signed, meticulous notes. Clearly, he's attentive to detail, and that's a crucial trait for a salesperson. If you are detail-oriented by nature, that skill translates to other positions. You will be a good mover, and you will be a good at sales. If you lack that trait, neither job is likely to work out for you.

"Don't put feathers on a fish," Oscar also warned me, and that, too, I've learned over time. Say someone is great at dispatch. He or she communicates well with the team and with clients. Suddenly, however, a need arises for an extra person in sales. A lot of companies would just transition that person over to sales, where good communication is only one aspect of the essential skill set. Such a move is putting feathers on a fish, but that doesn't make it a bird.

A leader must ask: Where does this person fit based on capabilities and desires? On my sales staff I have former service personnel who were in infantry and artillery, and one was a medic. Their backgrounds might not seem related, but I saw something in those people. They're naturals at sales for one reason or another. As the leader and as the manager, I'm there to continue to develop them. They've shown their stuff and earned that opportunity. I want them in the right place in our organization so they can continue to grow.

MAKING TOUGH DECISIONS

I have a sign in my office that poses three questions: (1) "Who did I say 'thank you' to today?" (2) "In this month, who did I look at promoting?" and (3) "In this month, who did I look at firing?" That last question isn't as pleasant to think about, but it is critical that a business put structures in place so that people answer to how well they're doing on the job.

An individual who hurts my brand could collectively cost us dozens of moving jobs through his malfeasance. Overall, that means we're employing several fewer people because we aren't getting the referrals and repeat business that comes from doing a great job. I'm the one who decides where to set the bar, and I set it high. For those who don't meet it, you can't work here. You have to go, because you would bring down the morale. You would hurt my company and weaken our brand reputation with clients.

"But that's someone's *life!*" some might protest. "He *needs* that job!" To which I respond: We all need our jobs. Someone who hurts my brand could cost us 100 moving jobs. That means I have to employ three fewer veterans because I decided to keep that one questionable person on our staff. When it comes to holding people accountable, sometimes it does get to the point of saying, "It's time for you to leave."

My dispatchers and sales staff have quotas. I clearly lay out my expectations. The paperwork must be correct. A minimum number of jobs are to be booked in a day. Those who do particularly well at hitting their goals get a bonus. It's a combination of carrots and sticks.

There was an incident a couple years ago at an air base in Afghanistan where some insurgents sneaked through the wire and ended up destroying four of our jets. The attack caused $200 million in damage. It was a huge loss to the Marine Corps—we lost about a tenth of our deployable fleet of that type of aircraft.

The two Marine generals who were in charge of that base and that area were both relieved of command. Some might say, "How was this *their* fault? How much could they really have done to prevent it?" That wishy-washy attitude of niceness fails to hold people accountable. Yes, those generals certainly had a lot more going on than just managing the individuals far down the ranks who should have been keeping guard, or their supervisors, or whatever the case might be. Nonetheless, the Marine Corps said, essentially, this: "No excuses. Generals are ultimately responsible for the base. It happened on your watch. You're out of here."

Perhaps other branches of the military are more forgiving, and it's rare that a general is relieved of duty. In the Marines, however, if you do not meet the standards, it's goodbye, whether you are a private or a general.

The Marine Corps places a major emphasis on accountability. You learn that from the start if you're a minute late for formation. Don't try to say the alarm didn't go off. You will be on time for everything. In fact, you will be early for everything, by 15 minutes or half an hour, because you know that's where your leaders have set the bar. That attention to punctuality and detail runs through the ranks. Every Thursday while I was on active duty, we had uniform inspection, in our dress blues or in our "Charlie" service uniforms. Every ribbon had to be perfect. It probably took me three or four hours to put together my uniform properly.

Every crease had to be exact. We measured the placement of our ribbons with a ruler. There are precise rules and specifications. Sure, we wanted to get out to the beach for the weekend, and it could seem that the lance corporal was just being a pain in the ass. But our leaders were holding us accountable. Marines are renowned for looking their best in uniform. Why? Because that standard, like many others, is set so high.

As a leader, I held my Marines accountable. I didn't just ask the troops, "Hey, do you fellows have all your water and ammunition for this patrol?" I made sure they did. With junior Marines particularly, I opened their pouches to be certain they had it all. A junior Marine might try to bring an empty canteen, figuring he won't need five pounds of water for an hour-long patrol. The leader sees the bigger picture, which is how that Marine will fare with that attitude some day on a long hump in the desert. What if the Delta Force and Army rangers at Mogadishu had tried that trick? Every Marine needs to understand that what's on his back could determine whether he lives or dies.

In war, a small mistake can lead to the loss of lives. The Marine Corps enforces discipline with the intent that it will become self-discipline. That's a trait that people should carry with them throughout their lives. We must pay close attention to the details, because it's the details that can hang us up.

A CULTURE OF CARING

The Marine Corps embodies a culture of caring. That might sound soft to those who want to think of it as a culture of hard asses who harp on minor details, but when you strip all that away and get down to the essence, you find people who are watching out for one another. They take care of their own.

That's the culture I want for my company. Some might say, "So, Nick, your goal is to fire one person a month?" They might see that as uncaring. It's actually the opposite. It's because I have high standards that the phone rings off the hook. If I don't keep those standards high, I could find our company losing prospects and jobs. That could mean we'd go from 100 employees to 10 employees—and how does that serve anyone's interest?

To terminate an employee is one of the toughest things a manager must do, but it will happen. If you are an entrepreneur with employees, that time will come. Remember that the greater good is to grow to employ the most people. Every time I make a decision, it's what's best for the company. It's not necessarily what's best for the individual. It's what's best for the group. If you keep weeding the garden, it grows to nourish more and more people. If you fail to do so—if you keep an incompetent friend on the payroll, for example—you are putting your business in jeopardy.

Every time I make a decision, it's what's best for the company. It's not necessarily what's best for the individual. If you keep weeding the garden, it grows to nourish more and more people.

Excessive niceness can be fatal to your company. You will encounter times when you need to make a preemptive strike. A lot of entrepreneurs struggle with that. I did, at first. But I have learned that those tough decisions are part of being a leader.

There is plenty of room for compassion. You need to know your Marines. You have to know what your employees are going through in life. Has a divorce or other personal issue sidelined someone? That's also leadership, to have that insight. You have to see the big picture every time. You have to do what works. You cannot be callous. Sure, you need to be the drill sergeant. You need to be tough—but to a point.

Let's say Smith is an hour late to work three days in a row, and a customer complained that he was on his cell phone for 30 minutes arguing with his wife. I might say, "Look, Smith, we've got to talk. Let me take you out to lunch so you can tell me what's going on in your life. I've been there myself. Why don't you just take a couple days off to think about things. Give me a call in two days and let me know if you're ready to come back to work." If Smith has been a reliable worker, he deserves that consideration.

Or maybe he doesn't deserve it. Let's say Smith hasn't been the most exemplary of employees. I might say, "Smith, I need to see you in my office now. You're holding back your crew. You're making it hard for my dispatchers. We have to keep putting out fires that you caused. Absolutely unacceptable. You're on probation for two weeks. Do anything wrong and you are fired. Do you understand?"

I've given that warning to employees who went on to become excellent workers. A leader must know which way to zig and which way to zag, depending on what the employee is going through and what would best get that person's attention. A leader must balance compassion against the greater need of the group and the business.

SO THAT WE ALL CAN FLOURISH

This is something that I certainly didn't learn to do at the University of Memphis. I am grateful for how much I learned there, but too many people see a degree as a magic key that will guarantee at least $60,000 a year after they send out one resume. A degree shows persistence, but it's just a first step. The finish line is out there in the real world, and it may be many years away.

One thing I know, en route to my own finish line, is that each of my employees is leading a life with plenty of day-to-day concerns. Many have families. Maybe they're going through a rough patch and need someone to cut them a break for once. Maybe they need a tough approach to get them to their senses. Far more often, what they deserve is encouragement and appreciation for a job well done.

When I can help an employee to succeed, I am helping a family; and when I am helping a family, I am helping the community. And in helping my community, I am serving my nation. Small business owners create most new jobs and those jobs increase the tax base.

When I can help an employee to succeed, I am helping a family; and when I am helping a family, I am helping the community. And in helping my community, I am serving my nation.

I am providing my employees, many of them veterans, with honest work. At the end of the day, they may be tired but they know they accomplished something real for their pay. About a third of my staff members are enrolled in school. This part-time job allows them to support themselves so that they can focus on their studies. It's another avenue for growth—and another means by which my company can help people.

Like ants in a colony, we each have a purpose. We each have a job, a role, a duty to the greater community, whether it is to our fellow Marines, our fellow citizens, or our colleagues on the job. Together, we are strong. Alone, we could not survive. We need one another, and we must watch out for one another so that we all can flourish.

CHAPTER 7:

....

A FRANCHISE ON YOUR FUTURE

Entrepreneurship is about self-determination. You are making the product or providing the service that you have decided is a good fit for you. With success, you become your own boss. You have gained independence and are on the way to financial freedom—and freedom from the clock.

Throughout history, most people have labored at the mercy of others. They were born into a feudal system, or into a caste, and their future was determined. Entrepreneurship, by contrast, is a reflection of our system of democracy and capitalism. As an entrepreneur, you determine your fate. You determine your own personal destiny.

That desire to find our individual destiny is deep in our marrow. Yes, we need one another, and we must depend on one another—each of us is part of the colony—but we also have an independent spirit. It's a spirit that is unmistakable in the Bill of Rights. It's a spirit that translates into constitutional debates and societal movements to protect the liberties of the individual. We've seen it politically for generations: women's rights and minority rights, gay rights and gray rights.

That spirit of independence is also what drives the entrepreneur. It's an itch. Like me, a lot of people are born with that itch. Some people discover it in school, some at their first job, or during their first enlistment, or first tour of duty. Some people find it when they are 40 or 50 years old—they get the itch then.

This book is for all those who have the itch. Perhaps you have an itch to start a business, or to take your business to greater heights. Either way, you yearn to succeed. It doesn't matter where you came from. That's the beauty of entrepreneurship. You don't have to start out as the general. You can start out as the lance corporal, or as the first sergeant, or as the captain. In the world of the entrepreneur, we all have the same footing. We face the same challenges and perils, and we also get the same opportunities.

The spirit of independence is what drives the entrepreneur. It's an itch. This book is for all those who have that itch.

EN ROUTE TO FREEDOM

As an entrepreneur, I know that my direct input is my direct output. How hard and how smart I work determines how much money I make. That can be risky, of course, because the opposite is also true.

I know a lot of business owners who make $80,000 a year, which here in D.C. is considered decent money. It pays the bills year after year. Then, if they decide one day to sell the business, they find that it will go for seven figures—such is the value not only of their assets but also of the brand and goodwill they have established. They are in a position to do what they want in life.

Their business, in other words, has brought them freedom, and it was their own decisions and savvy that got them to that point. As an entrepreneur, you set your goals. If you want to set your business up with systems at one location where you can work hard and make a steady low six figures a year, you can do that. Do you want to build an empire with a location in every major city in the United States? You can do that. You have a wealth of opportunities. Having a business can provide you a good income while it grows as an asset.

You're the boss: It's up to you to set aside the time and resources to accomplish your goals. That requires discipline and a keen sense of responsibility, but the rewards can be huge, and hugely satisfying.

A thriving business gives other people opportunities as well. You're building a company and you're giving other people a source of livelihood. Perhaps they will want to follow in your footsteps, and in so doing, they, too, will get their shot at freedom.

THE FRANCHISING ADVANTAGE

When I started Two Marines Moving, I created everything from scratch. I had to figure it out. It was like cooking without a recipe. Over time, I developed my recipe. I know the steps, in the proper order, and the processes that produce something good.

I intend to share that recipe. As my business grows, I have been exploring the concept of franchising. If other business owners follow the directions diligently, without getting distracted, they too should be able to produce something good.

You're the boss: It's up to you to set aside the time and resources to accomplish your goals. That requires discipline and a keen sense of responsibility, but the rewards can be huge, and hugely satisfying.

There is much to consider in granting others the right to use the name Two Marines Moving. I definitely see franchising as an opportunity to grow regionally and nationwide in small cities and big cities. Franchising will take my business into new territory. It's almost like starting another business, totally different from what I do now as I deal with clients for moving jobs.

In franchising, my customers will be other business owners, and I look forward to the opportunity to serve them and build the brand. I will need controls in place to ensure that our customers always get a quality product and that employees are treated well.

The mission must be clear and profitable. With a franchise, you typically have an upfront purchase fee into the system, and then you have a continuing royalty rate. Depending on the industry, that can be anywhere from 1 percent to 10 percent.

The benefits, however, are significant. With franchising, you don't have to reinvent the wheel. There's a system to follow. You have a support system. You have mechanisms in place. You know what your industry profit margin should be, and you know where you stand day to day and year to year. Franchises have a traditionally higher success rate than start-ups. With a franchise, your company is part of an existing ecosystem. It has a lower failure rate because you have guidance. You have a business *of* your own—but you're not *on* your own.

A good franchise is a turn-key system. I had to figure out myriad things on my own. With a franchise, you're given a step-by-step procedure to follow. Since it's a proven concept, it's harder to go wrong. You have that guidance. As long as you're in a good market for the type of business, your odds of doing well improve significantly.

With a franchise, your company is part of an existing ecosystem. It has a lower failure rate because you have guidance. You have a business of your own – but you're not on your own.

OPPORTUNITIES FOR VETERANS

I know that I am not the only person who got out of the Marine Corps wanting to start a business. A lot of entrepreneurs are former Marines. By starting a Two Marines Moving franchise, enterprising veterans will be able to build a successful business while providing job opportunities for their fellow veterans, the same as I do. A franchise will offer them a chance to create something for themselves and enjoy the many benefits of entrepreneurship.

There are many opportunities for veterans who are interested, and they can get help on a variety of websites, including VetFran and the Department of Veterans Affairs site. Such resources can be extremely valuable to those who avail themselves of them. Veterans may even be able to get a substantial discount on that initial franchise fee.

With a franchise, you have the training, support, and guidance that any entrepreneur needs. You can apply your skills, your savvy, and your leadership to a proven model. It's still your own business and your own success. You can put your stamp on the operation as the owner, if you are so inclined. You're not running some cookie-cutter operation. Your leadership and drive make all the difference. It's your baby. You pick the color of the tile. You hire and train the employees, and their success is your success.

Not that long ago, when Blockbuster stores were everywhere, I could walk into one and tell you right away whether the owner showed up very often. The floor was cleaner, the staff friendlier, the shop better organized. Your special attention as owner is what will keep the traffic coming back.

It is up to you to find the best mentors possible. For practical advice on how to run a business, I recommend entrepreneur networks such as the Marine Corps Executive Association. You will learn about events that you can attend where you will meet people who know the real answers.

Whether they start from scratch or purchase a franchise, veterans tend to be naturals in the business world. They have honed their leadership skills. The importance of teamwork has been drilled into them. They are accustomed to following procedures with precision accuracy. And they have come to appreciate the value of training. If you can follow a five-paragraph order in combat, you can follow a business and operations plan in business.

It's still a business, and you still face risks. Don't lose sight of that. But the risks are fewer when you are buying into a proven system—

and veterans are used to working in a proven system in which they have followed the rules and the steps. They understand the importance of processes. And they have seen by example what leadership is all about. As in the military, they are on a mission.

Veterans tend to be naturals in the business world. If you can pack for a 20-mile hike, you can follow a business plan.

CONCLUSION:

....

CARRYING
THE TORCH

In modeling my business after the great name of the United States Marine Corps, I know that I have a lot to live up to. The Marines have been around nearly 240 years. Two Marines Moving has been around more than six years, as I write this. The comparison humbles me, and yet I want to embrace the principles of that elite fighting corps and pass on its legacy. I want to create something that outlives me.

The Marine Corps is a relatively small branch of the services, and yet I know that I am among the ranks of innumerable brothers from many generations. Like them, I am a Marine forever by virtue of having served. I remind my employees that our clients think of us as Marines and that they have a dignified reputation to uphold, on every job, every day. It's that reputation upon which my success is built. It's because of that reputation that clients are clamoring for our service, to the point where I have to turn many away. But we will not grow for the sake of growing. I will continue to hire only the right people. People deserve to get what they expect.

The Marines emphasize that accomplishing the mission is paramount, even more important than the welfare of the troops. Many people in the business world proclaim that their associates are number one. I certainly care about my employees and their safety, but our mission is why we exist. If we're running late on a job, should we still stop for a leisurely lunch? Should we let a client wait so we can run a personal errand? If we neglect the mission, we all fall together. When the mission comes first, we all can rise to any occasion.

Leadership takes many forms—whether in the military, in business, or in family life. If you want to succeed in any endeavor, you must organize yourself and be in control of your life so that life doesn't control you. Entrepreneurs who become true leaders will find themselves profiting not just in dollars but also in the "pursuit of happiness" that the founding fathers held to be one of mankind's inalienable rights.

The principles for success that I have related in this book apply to any business, whether it's a moving company, a pizza shop, an automobile service center, or a fast-food restaurant. I could take what I've learned and apply those lessons to pretty much any other company, and I know I'd be successful. Each industry certainly has its nuances, but if you get the principles right, you're not going to go wrong.

That is why I have focused in this book on the bedrock for success. You need real-world information from people who are out in the field and doing this. Wherever you get your insight, look for those who have dirt on their hands—that is, those who have done and are doing what you want to do. You need more than an academic exercise.

Leadership takes many forms – whether in the military, in business, or in family life. If you want to succeed in any endeavor, you must organize yourself and be in control of your life so that life doesn't control you

Much of what I learned wasn't in a classroom but rather on the streets of Washington. I learned from things that went right and things that went wrong. By hooking up with people who have been there, you can learn from them how to avoid the mistakes they made. Learn from their failures as well as from their successes.

You'll no doubt want to attend a variety of conferences in your quest to learn, but remember that there's a lot of fluff out there. At some events, you'll hear speakers drone on about such basics as "if you want a loan, you need credit, collateral, character"—a lot of words, not so much insight. Instead, look for a conference of peers who can help you deal with real issues. "You're having a problem with an employee? Here's what you need to do." Or: "You're struggling with cash flow? I had the same issue, and here's what I did." You need to get real.

You'll be trying to clear many hurdles, and you will knock down a few along the way. Don't be discouraged. Go back and take another run at the ones that tripped you up. Soon enough, you will be making great strides forward again, toward the next challenge. When something slows you down or blocks your way, persevere.

As I write this, my company has made nearly 15,000 moving missions. In those moves, there are 15,000 stories. Whenever I can help a fellow veteran and add one more story of success, then I count myself a success. I love what I do. I was born to be an entrepreneur, and it is my pleasure to help others who are on the move, too. This is your moment to carry the torch.

APPENDIX: MARINE CORPS PRINCIPLES AND TRAITS

Following are the official Marine Corps principles and traits that every recruit is expected to take to heart. One or another of them is reflected on virtually every page of this book. After each, I have offered my perspective on what that principle or trait meant to me during my years of service and how it applies to the world of business.

MARINE CORPS PRINCIPLES

BE TECHNICALLY AND TACTICALLY PROFICIENT.

Marines seek to be the absolute best at what they do, and that should be a way of life in business, as well. I'm constantly reading and researching my industry to learn what we could improve.

KNOW YOURSELF AND SEEK SELF-IMPROVEMENT.

If you're fine with the status quo, then entrepreneurship is not for you.

KNOW YOUR MARINES AND LOOK OUT FOR THEIR WELFARE.

In dealing with employees, one might need a firm approach while another calls for some empathy. By knowing them, you can judge how to produce the result that's best for everyone, and for the company.

KEEP YOUR MARINES INFORMED.

Marines know the plan for the day, generally, and get plenty of feedback. I run my company that way, too. We post customer feedback for all to see, and we talk about the bigger picture: When people move, it's often because of some major event in their lives. We have one opportunity to get it right, and everyone must understand the objective and work together toward it.

SET THE EXAMPLE.

When other employers see "Two Marines Moving" on a resume, I want it to stand for something. I want them to think, "Wow, what a great company. If you worked there, that speaks volumes about you." Each job within the company is a reflection of the team as a whole, and how well we do will directly influence my workers' job prospects elsewhere. As we set the example, we grow as a company, which means I hire more veterans to continue that cycle of excellence.

ENSURE YOUR TASK IS UNDERSTOOD, SUPERVISED, AND ACCOMPLISHED.

This is as concrete and obvious as it gets. A good leader doesn't say, "Here's kind of what I'd like to see soon." A good leader says, "This is what we will do within 30 days." Then you build consensus by asking for input—and that's critical, because the front line will have the most useful information and feedback. A leader analyzes that information, sets the expectation, monitors the task, and makes adjustments along the way to getting it done.

TRAIN YOUR MARINES AS A TEAM.

In the Marines, everything is win or fail as a team. If a few Marines straggle in late on a hike, everyone fails the exercise. Then the leaders decide what could have been done better and what needs to be done now—such as, do some of the men need more time in the gym, or a special diet? In my company, if the lowest-level crew member doesn't submit a schedule, I tell the dispatchers in charge, "They failed, and guess who else failed. You did, and I did." It's a pass/fail system for all—no grades of A, B, C, D, or F for some. And when we don't pass, we figure out how we will pass the next time.

MAKE SOUND AND TIMELY DECISIONS.

Don't analyze all day long. You certainly need to gather data and strive to understand it thoroughly—but you need to do so expediently, as well. A 90 percent solution now is better than a 100 percent solution later. Get the ball rolling. Both in the Marines and in the business world, waiting and waiting for that 100 percent solution will lead to paralysis.

DEVELOP A SENSE OF RESPONSIBILITY IN YOUR SUBORDINATES.

We should feel accountable and responsible to one another. My company is pretty much booked up with jobs year round—not a bad problem to have—and I offer commissions and bonuses to my sales staff, in addition to their hourly pay. I get people to see how the sales, dispatch, and recruiting people depend on one another. How much they make depends on how well each does the job. Sometimes I tell the sales staff, "Look, if a crew is available but there's no job for them, then there's no pay for them. So if you can't find them a customer, how will they pay their bills?" Everyone's paycheck depends on everyone's efforts—and they know that's no bull.

EMPLOY YOUR UNIT IN ACCORDANCE WITH ITS CAPABILITIES.

Put the right people in the right jobs that suit their abilities. That's related to knowing your Marines—or your employees. Don't set someone up for failure. Someone who is great at sales, for example, might not be a great sales manager. Those are different skill sets. The manager certainly needs to excel at the task, but he or she also must be able to lead people effectively.

SEEK RESPONSIBILITY AND TAKE RESPONSIBILITY FOR YOUR ACTIONS.

Leaders delegate tasks, but not responsibility. When I was offered the opportunity to lead the patrol in Iraq, I was ready to go. If I'd made a mistake and things had gone astray, it would have been totally my mistake. Just as you own your successes, you have to own your failures 100 percent. When my construction business failed, I couldn't blame the housing market. It was 100 percent my fault. There always will be outside forces at play, and I could have taken steps to counteract them. Successful people own their mistakes, because that's the only way you can reflect and correct and get better results. They don't point fingers at anyone or anything but themselves.

MARINE CORPS TRAITS

DEPENDABILITY:
THE CERTAINTY OF PROPER PERFORMANCE OF DUTY.

At Two Marines Moving, we have a 30-minute arrival window, unlike many companies that tell you they'll show up sometime within a four-hour period. People end up taking an entire day off from work just for a service call. I saw there was a lack of dependability among other moving companies, and I vowed to be different. People consider Marines to be dependable, to do what they say they will do, and do it right.

BEARING:
CREATING A FAVORABLE IMPRESSION IN CARRIAGE, APPEARANCE, AND PERSONAL CONDUCT AT ALL TIMES.

Marines learn that in boot camp. After a 16-hour day and a 10-mile run, the Drill Instructor is in your face ordering push-ups. You're taught to still hold your bearing—to be unflappable, to keep in control. Even when you feel irritated or confused, you don't show it. You do what needs to be done and figure out the solution. Bearing means keeping your cool under fire—a worthy trait in any walk of life.

COURAGE:
THE MENTAL QUALITY THAT RECOGNIZES FEAR OF DANGER OR CRITICISM, BUT ENABLES A MAN TO PROCEED IN THE FACE OF IT WITH CALMNESS AND FIRMNESS.

It's normal to be scared in combat, but it must not stymie you. It can feel frightening when you start a business, too—and that's what stops so many people from trying. They figure guys like Fred Smith and Jeff Bezos and Mark Cuban must be fearless, but in truth they understand completely how it feels. They didn't let fear stop them. They had the courage to push through. And neither should criticism hold you back. In boot camp, when asked to explain why you didn't do enough push-ups or finish a run quickly enough or why you scored only a 96 on a test instead of 100, you are expected to respond, "No excuses, sir!" Then you say how you'll make it right and perfect next time. Failure is a step toward improvement, not an excuse to stop. You have to get over fearing what people might think of you.

DECISIVENESS:
ABILITY TO MAKE DECISIONS PROMPTLY AND TO ANNOUNCE THEM IN CLEAR, FORCEFUL MANNER.

This is a trait that I've emphasized throughout this book. A leader must be able to make command decisions, and promptly. Remember: a 90 percent solution now is better than a 100 percent solution later. Don't waste precious time in a state of uncertainty. Make the decision, make it clear to everyone who needs to know, and go.

ENDURANCE:
THE MENTAL AND PHYSICAL STAMINA MEASURED BY THE ABILITY TO WITHSTAND PAIN, FATIGUE, STRESS, AND HARDSHIP.

Keep pushing forward, one foot in front of the other. If you fall down, you get back up and you push forward again. You have to develop the strength of mind and body to keep to the task under adverse conditions. It's the mark of a good Marine, and it's the mark of a good businessman.

ENTHUSIASM:
THE DISPLAY OF SINCERE INTEREST AND EXUBERANCE IN THE PERFORMANCE OF DUTY.

When I communicate with my staff, I do so with high purpose and high energy. The way you say something can be as important as what you say, and enthusiasm brings power to your message. Whether you're giving a simple order or explaining a mission, show your own sense of commitment. That's how you invigorate people to greater accomplishment. That's the role of cheerleaders in sports. They're not there just to be good-looking. They're there to invigorate the crowd.

INITIATIVE:
TAKING ACTION IN THE ABSENCE OF ORDERS.

If you're a truly effective leader, you do more than run the ship right. The ship runs right even when you're not there. In the Marines, I faced high-risk situations. If a bullet found me, or a roadside bomb took me out, others would need to fill my role. They needed to be trained for such a contingency. They need to think for themselves and understand the mission. They need to recognize what needs to be done. The military is not about someone barking orders. It's a machine that can take a hit and still run smoothly without losing power.

INTEGRITY:
UPRIGHTNESS OF CHARACTER AND SOUNDNESS OF MORAL PRINCIPLES; INCLUDES THE QUALITIES OF TRUTHFULNESS AND HONESTY.

Marines and businesspeople must operate with unquestionable integrity. Without it, no organization can operate effectively for the long term. You must be forthright with people and give them the truth, not a shade of the truth. Marines do what they say they will do, with fairness and honesty—and that's our operating principle at Two Marines Moving. If we believe a job will take six hours to complete, that's the estimate we give—even if it's double the price of a competitor who lowballs at an impossible three hours.

JUDGMENT:
THE ABILITY TO WEIGH FACTS AND POSSIBLE SOLUTIONS ON WHICH TO BASE SOUND DECISIONS.

An effective leader must be able to evaluate all the incoming data and make the right judgment calls. The idea that you can "just keep pushing forward and keep at it" is brainless unless you weigh the information and push forward in the right direction. Marines survey the scenario—incoming fire, casualties, insurgents—and deal with first things first, all the while keeping the big picture in mind. Business leaders, too, must juggle many challenges and do what's right.

JUSTICE:
GIVING REWARD AND PUNISHMENT ACCORDING TO MERITS OF THE CASE IN QUESTION. THE ABILITY TO ADMINISTER A SYSTEM OF REWARDS AND PUNISHMENTS IMPARTIALLY AND CONSISTENTLY.

We deserve to expect fair treatment. Nobody should ever have to think their superior is playing favorites. A just leader will administer rewards and discipline based on an individual's actions, not on whether he likes that person.

KNOWLEDGE:
UNDERSTANDING OF A SCIENCE OR AN ART. THE RANGE OF ONE'S INFORMATION, INCLUDING PROFESSIONAL KNOWLEDGE AND UNDERSTANDING OF YOUR MARINES.

We must continually seek out knowledge. We must not remain stagnant. In the Corps, I took 35 optional tests on Marine procedures. I knew that if I were to be the best, I would need knowledge. You can't fake that, and when you possess it, others will respect you for it. I take that approach with Two Marines Moving. I try to be a sponge for new information on all aspects of the business.

TACT:
THE ABILITY TO DEAL WITH OTHERS WITHOUT CREATING OFFENSE.

You need to use different tacks with different people. Effective leaders often have "command presence." People listen. The approach of "do this, and do it now!" usually gets the job done, but it can go too far at times. There are other ways, and there are situations when a leader should try harder to get people to buy in. Sometimes that produces far more loyal cooperation and effort. There's a time for strict orders, but there's a time to train people to think like you do.

UNSELFISHNESS:
AVOIDANCE OF PROVIDING FOR ONE'S OWN COMFORT AND PERSONAL ADVANCEMENT AT THE EXPENSE OF OTHERS.

When I was in the infantry, the cooks would come out sometimes and deliver meals more special than the MREs, or Meals Ready to Eat, that have been an a warehouse shelf for years. When I was a junior Marine, I was one of the first ones to eat. As I progressed in rank, I was one of the last ones to eat. The food call goes by rank—and not as you might expect. The privates eat first, then the lance corporals, and so on. If there's anything left—and there should be—then the officers eat. I think that's symbolic of putting others before yourself. Leaders need to communicate that they are committed first to the interests of others.

LOYALTY:
THE QUALITY OF FAITHFULNESS TO COUNTRY, THE CORPS, THE UNIT, TO ONE'S SENIORS, SUBORDINATES, AND PEERS.

I no longer have any contractual obligation with the Marine Corps—but I still make all of my decisions bearing in mind that what I do reflects on myself as a Marine, and reflects on the Corps. As a businessman, whether dealing with a client or an employee, I want to treat everyone fairly. I want to uphold the reputation of those who came before me and those who are following. I feel that loyalty to the Marine family and all that we strive to accomplish.

Joining the military and starting a business both carry enormous risks. You can quickly find yourself in stressful, unfamiliar situations with both. However, you must remember that failure isn't an option. Our country has thrived for 239 years because failure has never been an option. The men and women of our armed forces protect us, provide for our security, and allow us to sleep well at night. Somewhere in the world, at any given minute, there are Marines, soldiers, sailors, and airmen standing guard. The second reason our country continues to thrive is because of our strong and resilient economy. It's not large corporations that act as the primary drivers of job creation, but scrappy and tenacious entrepreneurs who form the bedrock of our economic system. Learn from everything I've done right and wrong and take that next step. Be bold, take action, build your dream, and make your own destiny.